Life Takes Time

40 Lessons From A Life In Motion

What the Years Asked Me To Learn

Written By: Jesse J. Jacoby

Soulspire Publishing
Nevada City, CA, 95959

ISBN: 978-1-968660-33-8
Library of Congress Control Number: 2012921011
Dewey CIP: 641.563 **OCLC:** 213839254

Cover art, font, and layout are all original art by:

Wholesalers to book trade: Nelson's Books and Ingram

Available through Amazon.com, BarnesAndNoble.com

For Bambi,

Thank you for encouraging me, on my fortieth birthday, to write down the lessons my life had already taught me. These pages exist because you saw value in the years I had lived and reminded me to honor them.

Acknowledgments

This book would not exist without the many turns that interrupted the path I was on. Some came as lessons and others arrived as loss, resistance, or unraveling. Each struggle redirected my life in ways I could not have understood at the time but now recognize as necessary. What I perceived as detours became teachers and what once felt like endings became invitations to listen more closely.

I acknowledge every experience that shaped these pages. Both the ones I welcomed and the ones I resisted. The moments of clarity and the seasons of confusion. The victories that strengthened my confidence and the failures that softened my heart. Each played a role in slowing me down enough to notice what life was asking me to learn.

I am deeply grateful to those who walked beside me during times of uncertainty, and to those whose absence taught me discernment, boundaries, and self-trust. Even the difficult chapters offered wisdom, if I was willing to stay present long enough to receive the lessons bound within.

Above all, I acknowledge my children. You are my greatest teachers. Your presence continually reorients me toward what matters most, being integrity, patience, humility, and love. In watching you grow, I am reminded that life does not rush, and that becoming is not a race. Much of what I have learned, and much of what I am still learning, has come through being your father.

Introduction

From an early age, I wanted to know more about wisdom. Even during seasons of turbulence, confusion, and struggle, a quiet orientation toward meaning remained present in my conscience. Life did not unfold gently, yet a pull toward understanding persisted. I developed an affinity toward learning what mattered, choosing depth over distraction, and becoming someone trustworthy in the presence of difficulty.

Growing up brought moments that fractured certainty and tested resolve. Chaos, instability, and pain introduced themselves early, and often without explanation or guidance. Still, beneath those conditions lived a steady impulse to become a good person. I was not attempting to be perfect or performative, but simply someone who could stand in integrity even when circumstances encouraged compromise. My path to becoming this man was rocky.

That orientation shaped many choices. Some arrived consciously, and others instinctively. While my peers chased escape, numbness, or approval, my attention kept returning to purification of thought, behavior, and my body. Health became a language for me, discipline was a form of listening, and integrity was more of a compass than a rulebook.

Mistakes occurred as they often do and lessons arrived through consequences. Each experience carried instruction, however, whether welcomed or resisted. Over time, those experiences began to organize into understanding. Patterns revealed themselves, while causes and effects spoke clearly. Life taught me through repetition until learning finally landed. This was a process of ascending through what I refer to as sacred hoops. These are circumstances we get tested by through different forms until we embody the lessons.

My body played a central role in my education. Physical health revealed emotional truth, and energy reflected alignment or discord. When my choices honored coherence, vitality generally followed. When my choices strayed from inner knowing, my body responded differently. Purification, in every sense, became a practice of remembering my roots and my purpose. I started to acknowledge how balance feels, what clarity requires, and the demands of alignment.

Healing unfolded for me as a relationship with honesty. Every layer removed made room for something more essential. Each discipline practiced strengthened trust between my mind, body, and spirit. Through that process, a path emerged that was not forced or chased. Writing followed naturally as a means for expressing myself.

I started writing when I was fourteen. Words became a way for me to distill experience into meaning. Writing offered a vessel for integration. What once lived as confusion transformed into language and helped me deepen my understanding and channel my emotions. The energetics that felt isolating became shareable. Healing expanded beyond the personal and began to serve others. My teachings followed from lived inquiry.

Over the years, wisdom accumulated slowly. I often prayed to acquire wisdom, still not fully understanding what this meant to embody the wisdom I was seeking. I found what I was looking for through patience, living, and staying present long enough for lessons to ripen. Some insights arrived quickly while others required decades. Many asked for humility before clarity was revealed.

On my fortieth birthday, an invitation arrived to gather these lessons. This required me to pause and name what life had already taught me. Forty lessons emerged, each one shaped by motion, choice, consequence, and grace.

This book stands as a record of these teachings. I am not offering commandments or instructions, just reflections from one life in motion to another. Every lesson carries the weight of experience rather than theory, and each page honors how becoming takes time.

Life does not rush growth and wisdom cannot be forced. Integrity matures through consistency rather than intensity and healing unfolds when honesty leads. Writing becomes meaningful when rooted in lived truth.

These lessons remain unfinished, just as growth remains ongoing. The pages that follow offer what the years have asked to be learned so far, shared in service of reflection, resonance, and remembrance.

Table of Contents

Beyond the Instinct to Take - 12

You Are Empowered By Everything - 13

Lesson I: Life Takes Time - 15

Lesson II: A Sovereign Man Follows His Own Path - 19

Lesson III: It Hurts to Heal - 23

Lesson IV: Freedom Is More Than Being Out of A Cage - 26

Lesson V: There Is A Place the Light Reaches Only After the Soul Has Fallen Into Deep Silence - 29

Lesson VI: Nothing Tastes As Good As Being Healthy Feels - 32

Lesson VII: We Create the World We Live In - 35

Lesson VIII: We Release Impurities With Exhalation - 38

Lesson IX: Belief Precedes Transformation - 41

Lesson X: Our Body Is the Garden of Our Soul - 44

Lesson XI: Anger Is An Acid - 47

Lesson XII: Every Organ Is A Unique Organism - 50

Lesson XIII: Our Vitality Lives In the Gut - 53

Lesson XIV: Absorb, Then Diffuse - 56

Lesson XV: All Therapy Starts With Heliotherapy - 59

Lesson XVI: Food Is A Cosmic Messenger - 62

Lesson XVII: Presence Is a Portal- 65

Lesson XVIII: Depth Over Distraction - 68

Lesson XIX: Live In Harmony With Your Values - 71

Lesson XX: Honesty Over Convenience - 74

Lesson XXI: Show Up For What Matters - 77

Lesson XXII: Reciprocity Is In the Giving - 80

Lesson XXIII: To Live Compassionately In An Unconscious World - 83

Lesson XXIV: Release Others From the Debt of Your Pain - 86

Lesson XXV: Get Familiar With the Sacred - 89

Lesson XXVI: We Can Omit Chapters From Our Story - 92

Lesson XXVII: Mistakes Are the Soil of Transformation - 95

Lesson XXVIII: Dancing With Difficulty - 98

Lesson XXIX: Change Your Prayer to Improve Conditions - 101

Lesson XXX: Intention Is A Vow - 104

Lesson XXXI: Illness Is A Messenger - 107

Lesson XXXII: Live In Such A Way That the Earth Is Grateful For Your Footprints - 110

Lesson XXXIII: Be the Kind of Person Someone Will Write A Poem About - 113

Lesson XXXIV: There Is No Retirement For the Soul - 116

Lesson XXXV: The Gift of Undivided Attention - 119

Lesson XXXVI: Leadership Is About Authenticity - 122

Lesson XXXVII: The Most Revolutionary Act Is to Change Ourselves - 125

Lesson XXXVIII: Awakening Begins Within - 128

Lesson XXXIX: Be Rich In Eloquence, Not Force - 131

Lesson XL: Never Compete With Fools - 134

Our Obstacles Are Our Allies – 137

Author's Epilogue: Discernment Is Medicine - 140

Note from the Author - 143

About the Author - 145

Beyond the Instinct to Take

Much of human life has been shaped by a quiet polarity. We are familiar with pursuer and pursued, taker and protector, predator and prey, or hunter and hunted. This pattern appears natural, yet within human consciousness often becomes identity. We are taught to secure, compete, and move quickly enough that nothing we value is taken from us. In this way, life becomes organized around acquisition and avoidance, and presence is replaced by strategy.

What if there is a way of living that does not belong to either role? A way that neither takes unnecessarily nor lives in fear of loss. Elevated awareness reveals that we are not bound to operate within this pattern. We can step out of the reflex to grasp and into a relationship with life that is shaped by care rather than control.

Much of what has been normalized invites subtle forms of taking such as ownership without reflection, consumption without awareness, and exchange without reciprocity. There is another way to move, one that honors life as shared rather than possessed. In this orientation, fulfillment is not extracted but experienced, and connection replaces conquest.

This book is an invitation to step into that space. To live in a way that reduces harm, honors responsibility, and approaches life without the need to dominate or defend. When this shift occurs, the cycle of taking and fearing begins to loosen. What remains is a way of being that participates fully, without turning life into something to win.

You Are Empowered by Everything

Nothing can be identified that arrives without purpose. Every experience, whether welcome or seemingly unwanted, carries instruction. Each encounter, delay, and detour participates in shaping perception, strength, and discernment. Power is not granted selectively but is offered continuously.

What empowers is contingent on us. The same moment can weaken one person and fortify another. The difference is in our posture. When life is approached as an adversary, energy contracts, but if seen as a teacher, energy organizes.

Everything teaches. Challenge strengthens discernment, loss refines value, delay builds patience, and joy reveals alignment. Even resistance plays a role while difficulty sharpens awareness. Nothing is wasted when attention remains present.

To be empowered is to recognize that nothing stands outside the field of growth. Every moment offers leverage, each experience contains medicine, and all encounters ask for choice. This book reminds you where power already lives, which is in your breath, your attention, and your willingness to respond consciously.

Teachings attributed to Saint Germain often emphasized the creative power of spoken alignment: *"I AM is the full activity of God."* What we consistently affirm directs attention, which then shapes experience. When awareness is claimed consciously, life begins organizing around that declaration, and empowerment becomes participation rather than waiting.

You are empowered by everything, not because everything is easy, but because everything can be metabolized into wisdom. I invite you to read this book slowly, listen inwardly, and let what resonates strengthen what already exists within you. The path begins here.

Lesson I: Life Takes Time

In my younger years, I searched for answers the way many do, urgently, hungrily, and with the quiet anxiety that time might run out before understanding arrives. My nights were spent consuming self-help manuals, success blueprints, and stories of rapid ascension. Each promised a formula to compress time, hack effort, and bypass uncertainty. The message was subtle, but persistent, expressing that *faster is better, and waiting is failure.*

Coming from a family without inherited financial wealth, money felt abstract and almost mythic. Prosperity appeared to belong to a separate class of people who had discovered a secret passage the rest of us somehow missed. I wanted to understand how stability was built, freedom was sustained, and how ease emerged without collapse. I wanted evidence that effort could become reward, that intention could shape outcome, and that struggle was not a permanent sentence.

What those books rarely taught was patience. They spoke fluently about acceleration, leverage, and domination over time. My life, quietly and persistently, taught a different curriculum. Growth did not respond to force, wisdom did not arrive on demand, and depth could not be rushed without consequence. The most meaningful transformations unfolded according to seasons, not schedules.

Over time, a realization settled in my body revealing that nothing of lasting value arrives without waiting. This includes strength, clarity, trust, love, and wealth that does not hollow the soul.

This truth has been echoed across civilizations for thousands of years. Lao Tzu offered a simple instruction that counters modern urgency: *"Nature does not hurry, yet everything is accomplished."*

At first, such statements sound poetic, and even comforting, but they are also deeply technical. Nature operates by law, cells regenerate at specific rates, bones heal according to biological timelines, and soil requires seasons to restore fertility. No living system responds positively to impatience.

The path forward for me was only revealed once my compulsion to control outcomes began to loosen. Effort still mattered, but so did listening. Discipline was important, but humility mattered just as much. Action had value, yet restraint carried equal intelligence. When urgency softened into presence, life responded differently. This was not because effort increased, but because alignment improved.

Eventually, the idea of *making something happen* gave way to participation. Rather than chasing success, my attention shifted toward finding coherence. Instead of asking how to arrive faster, the question became how to walk well. Ancient traditions understood this distinction clearly.

Confucius taught: *"It does not matter how slowly you go as long as you do not stop."* The emphasis here was not on speed, but continuity. Systems, whether personal, relational, or economic, collapse more often from misalignment than from slowness. Progress that violates rhythm extracts a cost that is always paid later, and usually with interest.

Trust enters quietly when one stops demanding proof before the process completes. Trust in the unfolding, in timing that cannot be rushed without distortion, and that what is meant to grow will grow if given nourishment instead of pressure.

The closer life was observed for me, the more clearly a pattern emerged. If I paid attention, every detour carried instruction and each delay contained protection. Many apparent setbacks were quiet redirections away from paths that would have demanded betrayal of values or self. With enough distance, what once looked chaotic was revealed as orchestration. This recognition is ancient as well.

Rumi wrote: *"Why are you so busy with this or that or good or bad; pay attention to how things blend."* Meaning is rarely announced in real time. Coherence often appears only in retrospect, when previously disconnected moments suddenly align into a comprehensible pattern. Life is not explained while lessons are being lived. Meaning emerges after integration.

This book was born from that understanding. These lessons were not collected from theory or borrowed from ideology.

Each was earned through repetition, missteps, waiting, and return. They ripened slowly, demanding patience before clarity could arrive.

I learned that life does not rush instruction and time is the curriculum. Nothing living unfolds on command. Seeds do not respond to urgency, and roots do not grow faster when observed. The impatience of youth believes effort alone determines arrival. The correction of maturity learns that timing governs everything effort cannot.

Growth requires rhythm, light and dark, movement and rest, and exertion and recovery. What arrives too quickly often leaves just as fast. What is allowed to mature develops the structure required to remain. Life teaches slowly because depth demands time. Wisdom waits until the nervous system is ready to hold complexity without fracture.

To rush is to skim the surface and to wait is to enter the roots. Life takes time, as preparation.

Lesson II: A Sovereign Man Follows His Own Path

From early on, the world makes offers, and not all arrive as commands. Many come quietly, and dressed as opportunity, safety, or belonging. Expectations are framed as norms, incentives masquerade as freedom, and compliance is rewarded with comfort, while questioning is subtly penalized with uncertainty.

Long before a person consciously chooses a direction, the culture begins steering attention outward. Children are taught, often indirectly, that meaningful change belongs to someone else who is louder, wealthier, credentialed, or sanctioned. Vision is externalized and authority is outsourced. Over time, ambition shrinks from a living impulse into a managed aspiration.

When this belief takes root, creation is replaced by maintenance. A life capable of authorship settles into administration. Yet the truth is simple and rarely spoken, that if a person does not build what the heart imagines, the same energy will be spent constructing someone else's dream. Energy does not vanish, time does not idle, and labor always serves something. A sovereign man understands this early or learns through exhaustion.

This is not rebellion for rebellion's sake. Sovereignty is quieter than resistance. This is the refusal to offer one's strength to purposes that feel hollow, imposed, or misaligned.

This is the discernment to ask before committing the body and mind to any structure: *What does this work serve, and at what cost to my integrity?*

The ancient Taoists understood this danger well. Zhuangzi warned of lives lost not through violence, but through misdirection: *"The true man is not bound by what ensnares others."*

Ensnarement rarely looks like chains. More often, this looks like careers built on values one does not share, obligations accepted without consent, and roles inhabited so long they begin to feel like identity.

Sovereignty does not mean withdrawal from responsibility but conscious participation. The sovereign man does not ask only *Can I do this?* but *Should I?* Not merely *Who pays me?* but *Who benefits from my labor?* and *Does this work nourish the life I am meant to live?*

The Stoics approached sovereignty from a different angle but arrived at the same truth. Epictetus, once enslaved, made a distinction that remains radical: *"No man is free who is not master of himself."* External freedom means little if the will is continually conscripted by incentives that contradict conscience. A man may appear successful while quietly living as an instrument to be useful, productive, and replaceable.

To believe that one cannot change the world is to unknowingly consent to someone else doing so. To abandon ambition entirely is abdication. The world will be shaped regardless. The only question is whether one participates as an author or as a tool.

I have made a statement with my life, even having little resources, to be as productive as I can and to develop as many of my ideas as possible into tangibles.

Modern thinkers echoed this concern as systems grew more sophisticated. Simone Weil observed with piercing clarity: *"The danger is not that machines will behave like humans, but that humans will behave like machines."*

When efficiency becomes the highest value, the human being is reduced to function. Sovereignty erodes not through tyranny alone, but through convenience accepted without reflection. Claiming sovereignty begins with devotion to what you love. Love, in this sense, is orientation.

When work arises from love, effort becomes generative rather than draining. When action aligns with values, contribution carries integrity. When ambition is honored rather than suppressed, life responds with coherence. A sovereign man builds from the inside outward. Vision precedes labor and meaning governs motion. Such a man does not wait for permission to live authentically, nor does such a man confuse obedience with virtue.

The greatest theft is not of money or even time, but of potential quietly surrendered, one compromise at a time, until the original impulse to create is forgotten. Sovereignty is found in authorship. To love what you build is to reclaim your life. To build what you love is to change the world in the only way that matters.

Henry David Thoreau observed this with stark simplicity: *"The mass of men lead lives of quiet desperation."* This desperation is not born from poverty alone, but from misalignment, and arises when one's labor, attention, and creativity are consistently spent in service of aims that do not originate from within. Over time, this erodes vitality. The sovereign man recognizes that desperation is often the cost of delayed honesty, and that no external structure can compensate for an internal refusal to live one's own values.

A similar insight was later articulated through systems thinking rather than philosophy. Buckminster Fuller warned, *"You never change things by fighting the existing reality. To change something, build a new model that makes the existing model obsolete."* Sovereignty, then, is constructive rather than oppositional. I learned after working corporate jobs, then later creating my own schedule, that the sovereign man does not spend his life resisting systems he disagrees with while remaining dependent upon them. He builds alternatives aligned with his ethics, talents, and vision.

Lesson III: It Hurts to Heal

Healing is not always gentle. More often, healing arrives disguised as discomfort, pressure, strain, or a demand the body would rather refuse. This lesson was revealed to me in the early days of a prison boot camp, where my identity dissolved quickly, and our names were replaced with silence and numbers. During the first two weeks, we were called ghosts and dressed in whites and boots. The guards ordered us into stillness that stretched far beyond comfort.

For hours upon hours, we were commanded to stand at position of attention while facing concrete, with our nose and toes aligned with the wall. Posture was demanded of us where posture had long been neglected. For sixteen hours a day, my spine remembered a shape forgotten through years of sitting, collapsing, and bracing against life. Pain arrived immediately and was sharp and insistent.

Movement was forbidden, slouching was punished, and our meals were eaten standing, with time reduced to urgency. My body protested, muscles burned, bones ached, and every instinct asked for relief. I had to withstand the demands. Something unexpected occurred, however.

As the days passed, my awareness deepened. Beneath the pain lived correction. Beyond the strain lived alignment. My spine slowly rose, chest opened, and body relearned how to carry along with dignity. What first felt like cruelty was revealed as repair that was harsh and unrelenting, but undeniably effective.

Healing felt exacting and did not feel kind. My body was being mended by pressure rather than comfort. Years of imbalance were being addressed not through ease, but through insistence. Pain became instruction and endurance became initiation. This lesson extended beyond the body.

This principle is ancient. In Zen tradition, correction is not viewed as punishment, but as clarity. Dōgen taught that awakening is not an escape from the body, but a return: *"To study the self is to forget the self. To forget the self is to be actualized by all things."*

In forgetting the comfort-seeking identity, my body reentered truth. Posture corrected not just my spine, but the relationship to effort, presence, and responsibility. Alignment began to feel like integrity made physical. This law extends far beyond the body.

Emotional healing follows a similar law. Long-held patterns resist change and old wounds resist attention. To correct what has been misaligned for years requires passing through sensation that cannot be bypassed. Growth demands contact and healing asks for presence, even when presence hurts.

The early Greek physicians understood this well. Hippocrates observed: *"Healing is a matter of time, but sometimes also a matter of opportunity."* Comfort does not always heal and avoidance does not repair. Relief too early can interrupt restoration. Healing requires staying with the breath when the legs shake, adhering to the truth when identity dissolves, and enduring the discomfort long enough for integration to occur. Pain is the passage, not the goal.

I learned that what heals is not a form of suffering, but the willingness to remain conscious while passing through difficulty. On the other side of that endurance lives a body more upright, a mind more disciplined, and a spirit less fragmented. To heal hurts because healing corrects what has been out of alignment, and once restored, alignment allows life to move freely again.

Lesson IV: Freedom Is More Than Being Out of a Cage

Freedom is often mistaken for geography. A gate opens, a door closes behind, and the body moves from confinement into open space. Many discover, sometimes years too late, that leaving a cage does not guarantee liberation.

There were seasons in my youth when institutional walls defined the days. Inside those walls, a truth became impossible to ignore, that many who would eventually walk free were still bound. Their habits waited for them. Their addictions lingered patiently beyond the exit. Their alliances, identities, and reflexes remained intact, rehearsed, and ready to resume. The environment would reclaim them because the environment was never the primary captor.

Some carried prisons within their nervous system while others carried them in belief. The walls changed, but the conditions did not. Freedom was postponed because freedom had not yet been understood.

This distinction has long been recognized in Eastern traditions. Huang Po spoke directly to the illusion of external liberation: *"If you seek freedom, first free your mind."* A mind trained to obey fear will rebuild the cage wherever the body goes, while a mind governed by habit will recreate confinement even in open land.

Years after my release, while I was standing in a wide field where wilderness stretched without fences, guards, or visible limits, something unexpected occurred. There were no orders, clocks, or authority watching and the land offered no resistance in any direction, yet a quiet instruction arose from within encouraging me, *Now free yourself.*

The question followed naturally, *from what?* There was no cage here, no rule restricted movement, and no threat shaped behavior but the answer still arrived with clarity. My freedom was still incomplete.

My mind had carried restraints into the open. Old narratives continued speaking, fear still whispered, and conditioned beliefs continued to dictate my worth, possibility, and direction. I learned that the most persistent prison had never been external.

This insight appears repeatedly across wisdom traditions. Jiddu Krishnamurti articulated this without ornament: *"It is no measure of health to be well adjusted to a profoundly sick society."* Many walk freely while remaining governed by appetite, environment, approval, and expectation. A person may leave confinement yet remain enslaved to reaction, compulsion, and inherited stories.

A great lesson for me was discovering that true freedom begins when the mind releases allegiance to narratives that are no longer true. True clarity, I realized, is when thoughts lose authority over identity, fear is recognized as sensation rather than instruction, and beliefs inherited without examination loosen their grip.

Freedom matures only when sovereignty reaches inward. To be free is to choose consciously rather than compulsively, respond rather than react, act without the need to escape, and stand in open land without searching for an exit.

The ancient Indian sages understood liberation as recognition, not departure. Ashtavakra taught: *"You are not bound. Freedom is knowing this."* The deepest liberation is quiet and arrives when the mind stops insisting on stories that once protected but now constrain.

Wisdom taught me that when identity is reclaimed from habit and the inner voice speaks with honesty rather than inheritance, this is a higher version of liberty. Freedom is not the absence of walls but the presence of awareness. Awareness, once claimed, cannot be taken away.

Lesson V: There Is a Place the Light Reaches Only After the Soul Has Fallen into Deep Silence

Silence is often misunderstood as absence of sound, movement, and even meaning. Silence, though, is preparatory, not empty. There comes a point in every life when noise no longer instructs, words repeat themselves, advice circles, and solutions multiply without resolving anything. At that threshold, something quieter begins to call.

Those who have walked deeply into awareness have long pointed to this same threshold. Adyashanti writes, *"True silence is not the absence of noise, but the absence of resistance."* In that absence, the soul is no longer bracing against experience. Silence ceases to be something practiced and becomes something inhabited. What arises then is not a new belief or strategy, but a direct intimacy with what is already present. The light that enters here does not illuminate concepts but reveals reality as experience, unmediated and whole.

The soul does not reveal truth while competing with distraction. Only after the arguments fade, justifications loosen, and the mind exhausts all rehearsals, does silence settle deeply enough to become fertile. This silence is entered, often reluctantly, after loss, fatigue, or surrender. In that depth, the familiar self dissolves. The one who performs, explains, defends, and strives grows quiet. What remains is honesty. Light does not force a way into this space. Light waits.

The light that follows silence warms, guides, and restores. Once this place is known, silence becomes refuge, a teacher, and the doorway through which the soul steps back into alignment.

The kind of illumination that transforms does not arrive through effort or declaration but through stillness, listening without agenda, and allowing the nervous system to soften the grip on control. In deep silence, the soul remembers how to orient, intuition reclaims a voice, direction clarifies without urgency, and answers surface not as commands, but as knowing.

This is why many avoid silence. Silence asks for vulnerability, removes distraction's armor, and makes room for truths that cannot be negotiated. Yet within that space lives medicine. Only in deep silence can grief speak cleanly, purpose reassemble, and light reach what noise has kept hidden. This lesson is not about withdrawing from life but about meeting life without interference and letting clarity emerge rather than being forced.

Thomas Merton echoed this knowing when he observed that *"Silence is God's first language; everything else is a poor translation."* When the soul rests in stillness, language loosens grip, and the need to explain life softens. Silence does not answer questions in sentences. Silence dissolves the questioner. In this state, meaning is felt, direction emerges without effort, and trust replaces the compulsion to manage outcomes.

The years taught me to return to silence is to remember where wisdom lives. Silence is not withdrawal from the world but the ground from which right action naturally arises. Lao Tzu wrote, *"To the mind that is still, the whole universe surrenders."* Finding ways to surrender my mind through long episodes of adversity and grueling chapters of grief and struggle made a significant difference in my life.

In this surrender, the soul no longer strains toward light. The soul becomes transparent enough for light to pass through, and from that place, life is met not with force, but with clarity, reverence, and quiet strength.

Lesson VI: Nothing Tastes as Good as Being Healthy Feels

Most people have never experienced health. They have only met relief, the absence of pain, and the temporary quieting of symptoms. Health, as a measure of lived vitality, remains unfamiliar.

Many move through life believing fatigue is normal, heaviness is inevitable, and clarity is occasional. Bodies adapt to depletion so gradually that numbness feels like baseline. When discomfort fades briefly, gratitude is offered, mistaking neutrality for wellness. True health, however, is announced unmistakably.

Health feels light before thought, spacious in the breath, steady without stimulation, and awake without urgency. Once this state is known, comparison becomes impossible.

Hilton Hotema reminded readers that *"Disease is the result of obstruction,"* not invasion. When circulation is free, elimination is unobstructed, and the internal terrain remains clean, vitality is expressed without resistance. Health, in this view, is not something added but something revealed once congestion is removed. The body does not need to be forced into balance. Balance is the natural state that reasserts when interference is cleared.

The purist lifestyle is not an aesthetic or an ideology. This is a relationship with life force and the choice to consume what nourishes rather than what distracts. We eat for vitality rather than appetite alone.

To recognize food not as entertainment, but as information carrying light, rhythm, and intelligence into the body.

Living foods speak a language the body understands immediately. They restore communication between systems, clean pathways, and return sensitivity to sensation. Through this clarity, the body remembers how to regulate without coercion.

Dr. Sebi echoed this principle through a different language, teaching that *"disease cannot exist in an alkaline environment."* Beyond chemistry, this statement speaks to alignment. Mucus, stagnation, and acidification dull sensation and cloud perception, while mineral-rich, living nourishment restores conductivity and coherence. As the internal environment cleans, taste buds recalibrate, energy stabilizes, and the body begins to signal clearly again with requests rooted in intelligence.

Purity is often misunderstood as deprivation. In truth, what I have learned after fifteen years of living as a purist, is that purity is refinement and can be defined as the removal of interference so that vitality can move freely. I noticed when excess fades, sensation sharpens, and when burden lifts, energy returns.

Our taste changes when real health arrives. What once felt indulgent begins to feel heavy, and what seemingly promised comfort begins to dull perception. The body, after being accustomed to stimulation, develops discernment when nourished efficiently and naturally. Appetite then aligns with intuition and cravings soften into choice. Vitality becomes a reward.

To live this way is not to reject pleasure, but to elevate pleasure beyond the tongue. Pleasure expands into clarity, endurance, presence, and emotional resilience. Pleasure becomes the feeling of being fully inhabited.

I can write with certainty that nothing manufactured rivals this sensation. No flavor competes with coherence and no indulgence replaces aliveness. Once health is felt deeply, compromise becomes difficult. The body asks for consistency and life responds with energy. Health, I now claim with pride, is the taste of life without misalignment.

Lesson VII: We Create the World We Live In

Thought organizes perception. Each day meets us already shaped by what we bring. What the mind rehearses becomes familiar and what is recognized as familiar is welcomed as believable. What is believed quietly governs behavior.

Action follows belief. Every choice, whether spoken or withheld, taken or avoided, leaves an imprint. Small gestures accumulate and repeated actions shape pathways not only in the brain, but in circumstance. Life responds less to intention than to consistency. Energy precedes both.

The Buddha expressed this same truth centuries earlier: *"All that we are is the result of what we have thought."* Energy flows where attention rests. What is repeatedly attended to gains weight, momentum, and form. To guard thought, then, is not suppression but stewardship. A disciplined mind aligns with reality and not control. From that alignment, action becomes precise, energy is clean, and creation unfolds with far less resistance.

Before words form, and action moves, the body broadcasts a signal. Nervous systems speak to one another without language and environments respond to presence long before plans are executed. The quality of attention carried into a space alters that space.

This is why two people can walk the same road and live entirely different lives. One moves through the world braced, expecting resistance, and rehearsing scarcity. The other moves with openness, grounded in trust, and attentive to possibility. The experience, not the landscape, changes.

We are not separate from what surrounds us. We participate continuously. The environment listens, life answers in kind, and creation is already underway. The only question is whether participation is conscious.

Anaïs Nin wrote, *"We do not see things as they are, we see them as we are."* Perception is active participation. What we carry internally selects what becomes visible externally. When inner orientation shifts, so does interpretation, and behavior follows naturally. The world begins to respond differently because the lens becomes clearer.

Creation is subtle, cumulative, and rarely dramatic. A thought held repeatedly becomes a tone, and when sustained this becomes a posture, and if carried long enough this shapes a life. This does not mean blaming oneself for every hardship. Many conditions are inherited, imposed, or unavoidable. Even within constraint, however, authorship remains. Response shapes reality just as circumstance does.

What I noticed over the years is when thoughts are refined, actions simplify, and when actions align, energy coheres. When energy stabilizes, life reflects order. The outer world mirrors the inner climate.

To live consciously is to tend this process with care. Change begins quietly as we notice where thought leaks into fear, observe where action drifts from value, and feel when energy contracts rather than flows. We notice this in a single thought softened, habit interrupted, or moment met with presence rather than reaction. From these small recalibrations, entire worlds shift.

James Allen wrote, *"As a man thinketh in his heart, so is he."* This is not metaphor but mechanics. Thought impresses upon the nervous system, the nervous system conditions behavior, and behavior arranges circumstance. The world we experience is not constructed from thought alone, but thought is the architect that drafts the blueprint.

I discovered with the years that when my inner dialogue shifts, my perception follows. When my perception changes, reality for me reorganizes accordingly. We change our circumstances when we embody our desires.

Lesson VIII: We Release Impurities with Each Exhalation

The body is always cleansing. Even when the mind forgets, with every inhale, life enters. With every exhale, something leaves. Breath is a dialogue, not merely an exchange. The lungs listen to the state of the nervous system, and the nervous system responds to the rhythm of breath. Together, they decide what is held and what is released.

Yogi Ramacharaka, writing in *The Science of Breath,* described respiration as *"the most important of all the functions of the body, for upon it depends not only life itself, but health, vitality, and power."* He emphasized that true breathing is not about force, but completeness, allowing the lungs to empty fully so that the next inhale arrives naturally, without strain. In this way, breath becomes a continual cleansing tide. What is stale departs and what is required returns. The body restores balance through rhythm rather than effort.

Most people inhale deeply and exhale hurriedly. Attention goes toward accumulation. More air, more effort, then more doing. Purification lives in the space of letting go. Exhalation is where the body softens grip. Carbon dioxide exits and tension dissolves. Acidity reduces and the heart slows demand. The body signals safety within. Even emotional residue from stress, fear, and agitation begins to loosen when breath is allowed to complete each cycle.

Impurities are not always physical. Some are chemical, emotional, and a result of inherited patterns still moving through the tissues. Each conscious exhale escorts these remnants outward. This is why breath becomes medicine when attention joins. I am not writing of forced breathing or controlled performance, but simply awareness resting in release. Lengthening the out-breath, allowing gravity to assist, and letting the body empty without fear.

Paramahansa Yogananda taught that *"the breath is the cord that binds the soul to the body."* When breath is shallow or restrained, awareness contracts toward survival. When breath is free and unhurried, awareness expands and purification occurs on multiple levels at once. In yogic science, exhalation is not merely expulsion of gas, but the release of nervous tension, karmic residue, and emotional charge held in the tissues. Each complete breath gently unties what has been knotted by fear or habit.

Modern physiology now confirms what these teachings long held, that exhalation activates the parasympathetic nervous system, stimulates vagal tone, and signals safety at the cellular level. Breath has been cleansing bodies since the first organism learned to exchange gases with the world. When breath is allowed to complete, the body remembers that purification is continuous, quiet, and already underway.

A great teaching I learned through my life experiences is that holding breath mirrors holding life. When breath is restricted, thought tightens, yet when breath flows freely, clarity returns and the body welcomes release. Cleansing does not always require action. Often, cleansing requires permission to rest the jaw, lower the shoulders, soften the belly, and trust that letting go is safe.

With each exhale, the body practices surrender without loss. Something unnecessary leaves and what is essential remains. Breath teaches the simplest wisdom, that *what enters must exit, and what is held too long becomes burden.*

To live in rhythm with breath is to live in rhythm with renewal. Each exhale offers a small death, while every inhale offers a return. Through this gentle cycle, the body keeps a quiet promise to cleanse, balance, and heal with each breath. Utilizing breathing techniques helped me endure some of the most challenging moments in my life.

Lesson IX: Belief Precedes Transformation

Change begins when permission is granted, and rarely with action. Long before behavior shifts, our mind decides what is possible. If we want our habits to reorganize, belief establishes the boundary of effort. The body listens carefully to these inner declarations.

Belief whispers repeatedly and does not shout. What is believed becomes familiar and what is familiar gets comfortable. This comfort quietly resists change, even when discomfort grows unbearable.

Joe Dispenza echoes this when he writes, *"To change is to think greater than the environment."* Belief interrupts the loop of the familiar past. When the mind no longer rehearses yesterday's limitations, the nervous system exits survival and enters creation. New choices become available not because circumstances have shifted, but because attention has. The future begins to organize the moment belief stops anchoring identity to what has already been lived.

Many wait for evidence before believing, yet transformation asks for the reverse. The body must sense permission before adaptation occurs. The nervous system must feel safety before growth unfolds. Without belief, effort is exhausted, discipline fractures, and change feels like punishment. This is why so many attempt transformation without crossing a threshold.

Steven Covey paraphrased this truth from Talmud in practical language: *"We see the world, not as is, but as we are."* Belief is the lens through which effort either feels futile or meaningful. When belief aligns with values rather than fear, action becomes coherent. Transformation then is not a battle against habit, but a realignment of perception. The inner world adjusts, and behavior follows as consequence rather than command.

Behavior is modified while identity remains intact and habits are replaced while self-concept stays untouched. The old story continues directing new actions as belief reshapes identity. When belief shifts, resistance softens and the body stops defending the past. The mind loosens allegiance to limitation and energy reorganizes toward possibility rather than preservation.

This belief is a quiet conviction and willingness to hold a new orientation before proof arrives. This serves as a representation of choosing to trust the direction of growth even while the terrain remains unfamiliar.

Bruce Lipton reminds us that *"beliefs are more powerful than genes."* Biology does not operate in isolation from perception. Cells respond to signals generated by interpretation, expectation, and meaning. When belief changes, the body receives new instructions. Stress hormones then give way to repair signals, immune responses recalibrate, and growth pathways reopen. Transformation is not the body being forced to comply, but the body finally being allowed to respond differently.

Transformation unfolds when belief becomes embodied. The breath changes, posture adjusts, and choices simplify. What once felt forced becomes natural, and what required willpower now emerges as expression. The body cooperates because the mind has granted consent.

This is why healing traditions across cultures begin with faith in process. This requires carrying faith that movement is possible, repair is permitted, and life responds to alignment. Belief guarantees direction, not ease. When held patiently, this direction reshapes everything. One of the greatest gifts I ever offered myself was the capacity to change my biology of belief.

Lesson X: Our Body Is the Garden of Our Soul

A garden does not fail because weeds appear. Weeds are part of the landscape. Neglect, however, allows weeds to take over. Our body functions the same way. Impurities accumulate quietly through food that burdens rather than nourishes, thoughts rehearsed too long, and habits that once offered relief but now restrict growth. Addictions arrive as coping mechanisms in the absence of nourishment.

Over time, the soil compacts, energy struggles to circulate, and vitality thins. Cleansing is stewardship. To pull a weed is to make space for what was always meant to grow. Removal restores access to light, water, and breath. The soil softens and roots deepen. This applies equally to the inner terrain.

Robin Wall Kimmerer writes, *"Restoration is a powerful antidote to despair."* She reminds us that tending land is not about domination, but relationship. The same is true of the body. When we approach the inner garden with reverence rather than judgment, care becomes reciprocal. The soil is alive, so responds. The body responds because we are always listening and making necessary adjustments. Stewardship restores trust between caretaker and terrain.

Thoughts that diminish self-worth choke possibility. Behaviors that numb sensation block awareness. Substances that promise escape eventually demand payment. None of these define the gardener. They simply indicate areas asking for attention. Cleansing asks for honesty rather than force.

What no longer serves must be named. What disrupts balance must be removed. What drains life must be composted into wisdom. As impurities leave, sensation returns, hunger clarifies, and cravings soften. The nervous system settles into coherence as the body remembers how to regulate without interference.

Mental clarity follows physical purification. Emotional stability follows consistency. The soul is expressed more freely when the terrain is tended. A garden asks for presence. Daily care matters more than dramatic intervention. Returning repeatedly to alignment restores resilience. Even neglected soil responds to patience. When the garden is honored, life grows naturally.

Wendell Berry echoes this wisdom when he says, *"The care of the Earth is our most ancient and most worthy, and after all, our most pleasing responsibility."* Our body is Earth in miniature. To tend is to participate in an ancient agreement that what is cared for sustains life and what is ignored degrades quietly. Health returns through fidelity to small, consistent acts of care.

From my decades of research and applied logic, I know that systems regenerate when interference is reduced and inputs become clean. When toxins are removed, circulation improves. When excess is cleared, signaling sharpens. The body does not need to be instructed on how to heal but requires conditions that allow healing to occur. We must heal from the disease of excess to reach levels of optimum health. A garden thrives when we stop trampling the beds and begin listening to the soil.

To garden the body is to accept responsibility without blame. Seasons will change, and some cycles will be easier than others, yet each return to tending and every choice toward nourishment, rest, and clarity signals devotion to life. The soul asks for presence. When the garden is honored with patience and humility, growth becomes inevitable, and beauty follows without being forced.

There is no requirement for the soul to be fixed, and the body does not need to be conquered. Both need space to breathe. I invite you to free up space and allow this breath to happen.

Lesson XI: Anger Is an Acid

Anger has a texture and tightens the jaw, shortens the breath, and heats the blood. The body recognizes anger immediately because anger is chemical. Stress hormones surge, acidity rises, and systems designed for repair are redirected toward defense. What begins as an emotion becomes a physiological condition.

Anger also alters time perception. Moments feel compressed, urgency overrides patience, and the present becomes crowded with echoes of the past. This temporal distortion further strains physiology. The body cannot heal while rushing toward imagined threats. Thich Nhat Hanh named this clearly: *"Anger is like a storm rising in consciousness. When we are angry, we are not ourselves."* In that state, the body braces against a future that is not yet happening, draining reserves meant for renewal. Healing requires a presence that does not coexist with hostility.

I learned early in life that anger is an acid and acids do not discriminate. When anger lingers, internal terrain changes. Microbial populations respond quickly to stress chemistry. Certain microbes thrive in acidic environments, feeding on the byproducts of prolonged agitation and fear. Balance then shifts, while inflammation finds opportunity, digestion weakens, immunity dulls, and cells suffer quietly.

When anger rises, cellular membranes stiffen, mitochondrial efficiency declines, repair slows, and organs tasked with filtration and detoxification carry extra burden.

What should pass through begins to stagnate. Anger rarely announces these effects. Being mad feels justified, energizing, and often masquerades as strength. In truth, experiencing anger causes corrosion, not only in tissues, but also in intelligence. If anyone is encouraging you to get mad, rage, and scream, politely decline the invitation.

Neuroscience confirms that sustained anger reduces activity in regions associated with empathy, integration, and long-range reasoning. The organism becomes efficient at survival while losing access to wisdom. James Baldwin captured this paradox with precision: *"Anger, in the way that you use it, can eat you alive."* Anger metabolizes attention, oxidizes tissue, and fractures relational awareness. When anger softens, intelligence re-enters the room. What once demanded force becomes navigable through understanding, and the body responds immediately.

Clarity depends on coherence and insight requires openness. When the nervous system remains locked in threat, perception narrows and reaction replaces discernment. The mind then loops familiar stories rather than receiving new information. Anger feeds repetition, curiosity dissolves, and wisdom retreats. This does not mean anger is wrong. Anger signals boundary violation and alerts awareness. In brief expression, anger protects.

When anger is rehearsed, stored, or weaponized against the self or others, the cost accumulates. What begins as a signal becomes a toxin. The body requires resolution, not repression. Release neutralizes acid, breath buffers chemistry, and forgiveness restores balance of internal harmony. Letting go is biological intelligence.

An important lesson I like to share is when anger dissolves, microbes rebalance, inflammation quiets, cells resume repair, organs regain rhythm, thought expands, and compassion returns without effort.

Peace is regenerative. If more people embodied this principle there would be far less chaos. To choose calm is to choose clarity. Choosing clarity is protecting intelligence. Anger burns quickly, while understanding nourishes slowly. The body always knows the difference.

Lesson XII: Every Organ Is a Unique Organism

The body is a community. Each organ carries a unique rhythm, responsibility, and form of intelligence. Together, they collaborate to sustain life. When harmony exists, health is expressed effortlessly. When communication breaks down, symptoms speak on behalf of silence.

The heart does not behave like the liver, nor do the lungs reason like the kidneys, and our gut does not experience time the way the brain does. Each organ holds a distinct temperament. Some organs are steady and patient, filtering and repairing quietly day after day. Others are responsive and expressive, reacting quickly to emotion, stress, and breath. Each one listens for signals and responds accordingly.

The body is not a single organism moving through time, but a federation of lives. Organs are not passive components awaiting command; they are living entities engaged in constant negotiation with environment, chemistry, and emotion.

Manly P. Hall spoke directly to this truth, writing, *"Each organ is, in itself, a specialized intelligence, possessing a consciousness peculiar to its own function."* Healing therefore cannot be forced uniformly. What restores the liver may burden the kidneys. What stimulates the heart may exhaust the adrenals. Time allows each intelligence to respond in sequence rather than collapse under simultaneous demand.

True healing respects jurisdiction. Each organ has seasons of labor and repair. The heart requires rhythm, intestines require regularity, and nervous system requires intervals of safety. Time is the medium through which this coordination occurs. When pressure is removed, communication resumes. Organs recalibrate at their own pace, inflammation subsides, and function returns organically.

The liver remembers excess, kidneys remember fear, gut remembers safety, and heart remembers coherence. When life becomes demanding, organs absorb more than chemistry. They register emotional tone and adapt to repeated patterns. Over time, personality forms as response.

To relate to the body as a collection of interchangeable parts is to miss the intelligence. To relate to the body as a living council invites cooperation. Healing accelerates when organs are addressed with respect. What restores one organ may burden another. What calms the nervous system may liberate digestion. What strengthens circulation may awaken clarity. True care listens rather than imposes.

Hilton Hotema extended this understanding into physiology and longevity, reminding readers and students that the body is sustained by cooperation rather than domination. *"The organs of the body are individual lives,"* he wrote, *"and health depends upon their harmonious relationship."* When life is rushed, this harmony fractures.

One system is pushed ahead while another lags, creating compensation rather than coherence. Degeneration often begins with impatience, asking organs to perform without adequate recovery, nourishment, or rest between cycles.

When nourishment arrives in forms the body recognizes, organs soften their defenses. When toxins leave, organs regain trust. When stress chemistry subsides, organs resume conversation. Listening becomes the medicine.

As awareness grows, relationship deepens. The body becomes our ally rather than obstacle and care becomes responsive rather than reactive. Every organ seeks balance, desires rhythm, and participates in wisdom. The body asks to be understood to restore harmony. When I acknowledged each of my organs as individual entities and developed stronger relationships with them, my life improved.

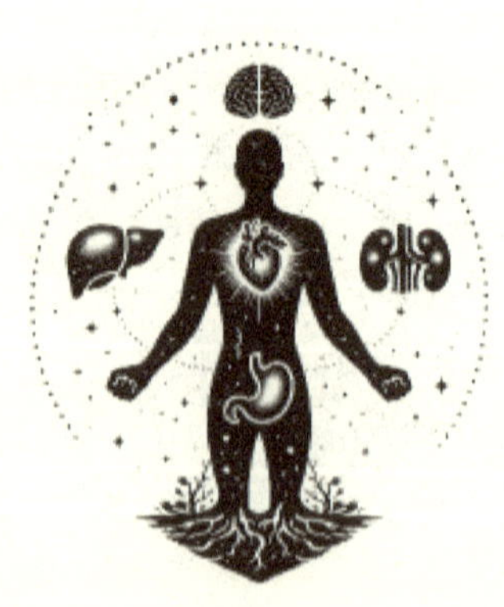

Lesson XIII: Our Vitality Lives in the Gut

Vitality begins in assimilation. The gut is where life decides whether nourishment becomes energy or burden. Long before clarity reaches the mind, the digestive system has already cast a vote. When the gut thrives, vitality rises quietly and steadily. When the gut falters, fatigue speaks.

The gut is not merely a digestive tube but a living ecosystem whose diversity determines resilience. Monoculture weakens all systems, including the body. Dr. Zach Bush speaks often to this ecological truth, noting that *"Health is a measure of biodiversity."* When microbial diversity declines, inflammation rises, immunity narrows, and vitality thins. Highly processed diets simplify the inner terrain, while plant-rich, fiber-diverse nourishment restores complexity. Diversity in food creates diversity in microbes, and diversity in microbes creates options for adaptation. Vitality depends on optionality.

Most people search for energy in stimulation. Caffeine, sugar, drugs, urgency, and adrenaline temporarily mask depletion. These borrowed energies never last. True vitality emerges only when the gut is supported, rested, and respected. When I learned how to nourish my gut, my vitality peaked.

Plant-based nourishment offers a unique advantage because plants arrive with complexity intact. Polyphenols, resistant starches, soluble and insoluble fibers, and living enzymes create layered conversations within the gut.

Michael Pollan summarized this ecological simplicity with precision: *"Eat food. Not too much. Mostly plants."* This is not ideology but biology. Plants invite collaboration rather than domination. When the gut ecosystem is fed consistently with whole, varied plant foods, vitality emerges as a natural consequence, not a pursued outcome. Energy stabilizes because the internal environment has regained coherence.

The gut is a sensing organ and decision-maker. Here, nutrients are chosen or rejected, immunity is trained, and microbes negotiate harmony. The gut listens constantly to what arrives, whether through food, emotion, stress, or rhythm, and responds accordingly. When digestion is clear, energy circulates freely. When burdened, vitality is redirected toward defense.

The body does not waste energy without reason. Survival always precedes expression. This is why healing so often begins in the belly. When the gut is inflamed, thought becomes reactive. If imbalanced, mood becomes unstable. When exhausted, the will weakens. Intelligence dims from lack of fuel, not an absence of knowledge.

Living foods carry order, fiber feeds harmony, and simplicity reduces friction. As microbial communities rebalance, inflammation softens. As a result, energy returns, and motivation follows naturally.

Research into the microbiome consistently demonstrates that fiber is not food for humans alone, but for the trillions of organisms that govern energy extraction, immune signaling, and neurotransmitter production. As described in *The Secret Life of the Microbiome, "Microbes do not simply digest food for us; they decide what kind of body we inhabit."* Short-chain fatty acids produced through plant fiber fermentation reduce inflammation, strengthen the gut barrier, and improve mitochondrial efficiency. Energy, then, is not something we consume directly, but something microbes help generate through cooperation.

Vitality is permitted, not forced. The gut teaches patience and responds to consistency rather than intensity. Bloating, craving, discomfort, and aversion are signals. The gut communicates in sensation. To ignore these messages is to delay vitality and to honor them is to accelerate repair.

Lesson XIV: Absorb, Then Diffuse

Life moves through us whether we are ready or not. Experiences arrive unfiltered and can bring joy, grief, pressure, beauty, and confusion. The question is never whether something will be felt, but whether we hold on.

Absorption is unavoidable but diffusion is a choice. To absorb is to acknowledge what is present without resistance. Sensation enters, emotion registers, and information is received. Nothing is denied or exaggerated. The body is allowed to feel what is occurring. This is honesty.

The nervous system is designed to complete cycles. Sensation rises, energy mobilizes, and resolution follows when experience is allowed to move through. Distress lingers not because something difficult was felt, but because the process was interrupted before integration occurred. Physicist David Bohm observed, *"In the implicate order everything is flowing and changing."* Absorption without diffusion traps energy, while diffusion without absorption bypasses truth. Health requires both in sequence.

Diffusion follows absorption. What does not belong is released, what is not needed passes through, and what cannot serve growth is allowed to dissolve. This is discernment. Many suffer because of what they retain. Feelings unacknowledged stagnate and those which are acknowledged move. When emotion is met directly, this completes a cycle naturally. When suppressed or rehearsed, this becomes identity.

Absorb, then diffuse. This rhythm has been my motto for years and keeps my center clear. Challenges lose their power when they are permitted entry without becoming residence. Pain softens when welcomed briefly and released consciously. Even grief, when honored fully, knows when to depart. This principle mirrors the body's own intelligence.

Emotional digestion mirrors physiological digestion. What is chewed thoroughly can be assimilated, while what is swallowed whole causes distress. The practice of mindful presence allows experience to be metabolized rather than stored. Thich Nhat Hanh taught this simply: *"Feelings come and go like clouds in a windy sky. Conscious breathing is my anchor."* Breath assists diffusion by signaling safety and reminding the body that movement is allowed.

Nutrients are absorbed and waste is eliminated. What is kept nourishes, while what is released restores balance. The same law governs emotional and mental health. Not everything that touches us must be carried forward, while not every story deserves repetition. Centering arises from trust in this process. By absorbing without judgment and diffusing without attachment, equilibrium returns, the nervous system steadies, perspective widens, and response replaces reaction.

Modern culture trains accumulation rather than release. Stories are rehearsed, grievances are preserved, and identity forms around unresolved emotion. Biology, however, favors flow. Bruce Lipton observed, *"Perception controls biology."* When perception becomes fixed, physiology follows. When perception remains fluid, the body retains flexibility. Absorb what informs growth and diffuse what constricts vitality. The distinction is subtle but decisive.

Ancient wisdom traditions recognized this law long before modern science provided a label. Rumi wrote, *"Try not to resist the changes that come your way. Instead, let life live through you."* To absorb and then diffuse is to allow life passage without possession. Experience is honored without becoming burden. Movement continues, coherence remains, and the self stays permeable rather than defended.

Lesson XV: All Therapy Starts with Heliotherapy

Long before clinics, prescriptions, and protocols, healing began with light. Human beings evolved beneath the sun where skin learned to read daylight and our cells responded to warmth, rhythm, and spectrum. Our nervous system calibrated by dawn and dusk and health unfolded in conversation with the sky.

Heliotherapy, or healing through sunlight, was once common knowledge. Ancient cultures would build dwellings around solar orientation and their temples welcomed light deliberately. Physicians prescribed sunlight for weakness, infection, melancholy, and disease. People recovered through alignment rather than intervention.

In the early days of modern medicine, sunlight was still understood as medicine. Patients with tuberculosis were wheeled outdoors and children with rickets were exposed to open air and sun. Wounds healed faster, immunity strengthened, spirits lifted, and light instructed the body.

The physician who formally reintroduced sunlight as medicine did so through observation. Auguste Rollier, widely regarded as the founder of modern heliotherapy, documented dramatic recoveries by restoring patients to daily, graduated sun exposure. He wrote, *"Sunlight is the most powerful healing agent at our disposal."*

Rollier understood that light was not merely a disinfectant or stimulant, but an organizing force. When sunlight met skin, the body recalibrated mineral metabolism, bone formation, immune response, and mood without coercion.

Often, healing requires remembering what has been forgotten. The sun invites coherence, as exposure signals safety to the nervous system. In safety, repair begins, sleep deepens, inflammation softens, and vitality returns gradually and without strain.

Sunlight activates processes no laboratory can replicate. Hormones synchronize, circadian rhythm resets, blood chemistry shifts toward balance, and cells receive information as much as energy. The body remembers how to regulate when light arrives at the right time, in the right measure. Healing does not always require complexity.

This is why absence of light correlates with illness. When the body loses the primary timekeeper, confusion follows, hormones drift, energy fragments, and mood dims. The body waits for instruction that never arrives.

We experience heliotherapy when morning light awakens purpose, midday light strengthens resilience, and evening light prepares rest. The sun teaches pacing, patience, and rhythm and reminds the body that life unfolds in cycles, not commands. All therapy begins here because light restores orientation.

Before supplements, techniques, and strategies, the body asks for clarity of signal. Stand in the sun and let the skin receive information. Allow the body to remember this ancient teacher. Healing follows alignment and alignment begins with light.

Living systems also store light. Plants receive solar energy and convert this power into structured nourishment that the body can recognize without confusion. Aris Latham speaks to this directly, teaching that *"Living foods carry the intelligence of the sun."*

This intelligence arrives intact through fresh fruits, greens, and sprouted seeds, offering energy that does not require stimulation or strain. When the body is nourished by foods and rhythms shaped by sunlight, vitality becomes steady rather than volatile. Energy no longer spikes and crashes when sourced from nature and not extracted.

My invitation for you is to nourish your essence by learning more about biophotons in your food and how our dietary choices play a supreme role in health and well-being.

Lesson XVI: Food Is a Cosmic Messenger

Food begins in light. Long before nourishment reaches the plate, energy travels across vast distances. Starlight moves through space, touches the sun, filters through atmosphere, and lands upon leaf and fruit. Photosynthesis translates that light into form. Geometry organizes growth, minerals rise from soil, water carries memory, and time completes the work.

Long before modern science quantified nutrients, observers of life recognized that food carries formative intelligence. Rudolf Steiner described nourishment as a mediator between cosmic forces and human physiology, noting that *"The plant world is the earthly image of the cosmic world."* What grows upward toward light gathers more than calories. Shape, color, fragrance, and structure emerge from dialogue between sun, soil, and time. When consumed, this dialogue continues within the body. Eating becomes an act of receiving order that already knows how to assemble life.

What arrives as food is condensed cosmos. Each living plant carries information shaped by place, season, and rhythm. The body does not merely digest this information but also listens. Cells receive instruction, systems adjust, and intelligence recognizes familiar patterns written into life long before language.

This is why living foods feel different. They carry order rather than noise, offer coherence over stimulation, and deliver vitality rather than demand digestion. When food is close to origin, the message remains clear. When overly altered, stripped, or engineered, the messages in food become distorted. The body then works harder to interpret what no longer resembles nourishment and eating becomes translation.

Food that carries life force communicates with clarity. The nervous system settles, gut harmonizes, energy distributes evenly, thought sharpens without urgency, and mood stabilizes without effort. This exchange is sacred, whether acknowledged or not.

To eat consciously is to participate in an ancient dialogue. Light enters plant, plant enters body, and body becomes vessel for energy that once traveled through stars. In this way, nourishment is continuation. Food remembers source and the body remembers how to receive.

When eating aligns with life force, appetite becomes intuitive, cravings soften, and excess loses appeal. The body chooses simplicity because simplicity speaks clearly. This is a great example of attunement. Food teaches timing, patience, and respect. Growth cannot be rushed and ripeness cannot be faked. Nourishment arrives when conditions are honored. A well-balanced plant-based diet offers life force paired with the complete spectrum of nutrients we require.

Every meal offers instruction and each bite carries signal. To eat well is to listen deeply to land, light, and body. When listening is restored, nourishment transcends calories and becomes communion. Food is a cosmic messenger, and the body is fluent when allowed to remember.

Physics echoes this same truth from another angle. Richard Feynman once reflected that *"The atoms that make up our bodies were once in stars."* Food is the pathway through which those atoms reenter living form. The body is not separate from the universe but is one of the expressions, temporarily organized.

When nourishment remains close to origin, being whole, living, and minimally altered, the message remains intelligible. Energy flows without confusion because the body recognizes history within what is eaten. This is a perfect time to improve your lifestyle.

Lesson XVII: Presence Is a Portal

Spiritual traditions have long recognized presence as the threshold through which life becomes intelligible. Thich Nhat Hanh reminded students that *"The present moment is the only moment available to us and is the door to all moments."* When attention leaves the present, the door closes. Anxiety then multiplies, clarity dims, and the body braces against imagined futures or unfinished pasts. When attention returns, the door opens again, and life resumes invitation.

Substance is not what we possess, but the quality of our presence. Nothing meaningful opens without arrival. The body may be in one place while attention remains elsewhere, whether rehearsing the past, negotiating the future, or fragmenting the moment. In such states, life passes by unnoticed, even when abundance surrounds us.

Modern culture rewards speed and distraction, yet presence remains the great equalizer. Eckhart Tolle observed, *"Realize deeply that the present moment is all you ever have."* In presence, decisions simplify, suffering loses momentum, and guidance becomes accessible without force. The portal opens through arrival. When attention arrives fully, life meets us there.

Presence gathers what distraction scatters. When attention settles fully into the now, something subtle shifts, time loosens, and the urgency to accumulate fades. What remains is alive, responsive, and sufficient. The moment begins to reveal depth previously obscured by haste.

This is where substance lives, not in objects, status, or possession but when attention is undivided. A conversation deepens, a meal nourishes beyond sustenance, and a breath restores orientation. When I am present in every moment I feel content with where I am at and no longer question my circumstances. I trust that I am exactly where I need to be.

Presence is the condition under which life can be metabolized rather than merely endured. When attention inhabits the body, sensation becomes intelligible and experience completes instead of lingering unresolved. Jon Kabat-Zinn articulated this with grounded clarity: *"You cannot stop the waves, but you can learn to surf."* Presence changes the relationship to difficulty. The body no longer braces against experience, and awareness no longer resists what is occurring. In this openness, life moves through rather than piling up, and presence is proven as capacity.

What is simple becomes profound when presence inhabits fully. The body recognizes this instantly, breath slows, muscles soften, and the nervous system releases vigilance. In presence, life feels less like something to manage and more like something to participate in. Meaning is no longer chased but is encountered. Presence is generous.

When presence is offered to another, trust forms without effort. When extended inward, healing begins quietly. When offered to life, guidance appears without command. The portal opens through stillness. Nothing needs to be added or proven.

Only attention must arrive. Substance is not what is held in the hands, but what is held in awareness. Awareness, once stabilized, becomes home.

Presence is not a mental posture but a physiological state. When attention rests where the body is, coherence replaces fragmentation. William James named this foundational truth plainly: *"My experience is what I agree to attend to."*

Attention organizes reality. What is attended to gains texture, meaning, and consequence, while what is ignored withers into abstraction. Presence restores agency by returning authorship to awareness. This is an invitation for you to broaden your awareness about how important your presence is.

Lesson XVIII: Depth Over Distraction

Distraction is engineered and rarely accidental. Attention is fragmented slowly, one interruption at a time. What begins as convenience becomes habit and habit reshapes perception. Depth erodes not through catastrophe, but through neglect. For something to increase in depth requires time, but distraction often consumes our time.

Philosophers of the present moment describe distraction as exhaustion disguised as freedom. Byung-Chul Han noted, *"Attention is the new scarcity."* When attention is constantly harvested, the capacity for depth withers. Depth requires protecting attention from being endlessly claimed. This protection is not withdrawal from life, but discernment about what is allowed to enter. Boundaries become the architecture through which meaning can grow.

The surface offers speed, stimulation, and endless novelty. Depth offers intimacy, understanding, and transformation. One excites briefly and the other nourishes slowly. Most never choose distraction consciously. Distraction feels like relief, dulls discomfort, fills space, and postpones listening, yet never satisfies.

Depth has always been preserved by those willing to protect silence. Thomas Merton wrote, *"Our real journey in life is interior; it is a matter of growth, deepening, and of an ever-greater surrender to the creative action of love and grace in our hearts."*

Depth is interior commitment that grows when space is defended from noise and when attention is allowed to settle long enough to be shaped. In this stillness, meaning clarifies, values consolidate, and life regains density. Distraction scatters the self, but depth gathers coherence.

In my younger years I would often decline invitations to go to parties and social gatherings because I wanted to work on myself. I chose instead to run sprints, write, and deepen.

After the noise fades, emptiness remains unchanged. Meaning does not emerge from constant engagement but arrives through sustained attention. Depth forms where presence remains uninterrupted. A single conversation carried fully, craft practiced patiently, and truth explored beyond convenience are acts of devotion.

Writers who live close to attention understand depth as a form of devotion. Annie Dillard wrote, *"How we spend our days is, of course, how we spend our lives."* Depth is a daily posture built through how one listens, reads, and practices a craft. Life thickens where attention is sustained.

Depth asks for courage. To stay with something long enough to understand is to risk being changed. Distraction offers safety through avoidance while depth offers growth through encounter. Choosing depth reclaims agency. Attention becomes intentional, thought sharpens, emotional resilience strengthens, and life feels less scattered and more coherent. This choice requires discernment.

Modern critics of industrial culture understood that distraction is a structural condition. Ivan Illich warned that tools meant to serve life often end up reshaping, writing that *"Neither revolution nor reformation can ultimately change a society; rather, you must tell a new powerful story."* Distraction is sustained by stories of urgency, productivity, and constant availability. Depth begins when a different story is chosen where attention is deliberately invested.

Every invitation does not deserve attention and not every voice warrants response. Each stimulus does not require engagement. Depth grows when boundaries are honored. To choose depth is to choose relationship over consumption, meaning over momentum, and substance over spectacle. In depth, life slows enough to speak clearly, wisdom matures, and the self remembers what matters.

Lesson XIX: Live in Harmony with Your Values

Values are practices. Many speak of what matters while living otherwise. The dissonance is rarely intentional and forms gradually through convenience, fear, or the slow erosion of attention. Over time, misalignment becomes normalized, discomfort fades, and integrity dulls, yet the body keeps score.

Integrity begins with governance of the inner world. Epictetus framed this with precision: *"First say to yourself what you would be; and then do what you have to do."* Values lose force when they remain abstract. Alignment occurs when identity and action converge. When a man knows what he stands for, decision-making simplifies because the answer is already present. Harmony is not found through constant evaluation but through prior clarity.

When actions drift from values, energy fragments. The nervous system senses contradiction, fatigue increases, motivation weakens, and clarity blurs because coherence has been compromised. Harmony restores vitality. To live in harmony with values is to remove internal conflict. Choice becomes simpler, direction stabilizes, and life no longer pulls in opposing directions. This alignment requires honesty.

The danger of misalignment is subtle and rarely announced as crisis. This appears as compromise justified by practicality. Ralph Waldo Emerson warned against this erosion plainly: *"What you do speaks so loudly that I cannot hear what you say."*

Values are not affirmed by language but by repetition. Each choice trains the nervous system either toward trust or fragmentation. Harmony emerges when behavior becomes a clear extension of belief. What is valued must be named, lived and protected.

Values are revealed most during pressure. In moments of decision, alignment or avoidance becomes visible, and the body responds immediately to either choice. When action honors value, relief follows, even when difficulty remains. When action violates value, discomfort lingers, even if success appears.

Consistency is the quiet proof of values embodied. Marcus Aurelius reminded himself, *"Waste no more time arguing about what a good man should be. Be one."* Values clarify when action replaces deliberation. When behavior aligns repeatedly with what matters, the nervous system settles into trust. Life simplifies because fewer internal negotiations are required. Harmony emerges through follow-through. What is lived consistently becomes character, and character becomes direction.

Harmony is felt, not argued. Living in alignment restores trust in self, intuition, and direction. Life responds differently when integrity is consistent. Obstacles clarify, support emerges, and effort feels purposeful rather than draining. This is resonance.

Values are truths discovered through experience, not rules imposed from outside. Once discovered, ignoring them costs energy. Harmony is steady, not loud. To live this way is to simplify life without shrinking. When values guide action, the path becomes clear, because direction no longer wavers.

Mythology understood alignment as destiny lived rather than fate imposed. Joseph Campbell observed, *"The privilege of a lifetime is being who you are."* This privilege is protected through daily choices that honor what matters most. When values guide behavior consistently, direction ceases to wobble. One no longer negotiates with oneself and life feels trustworthy again being lived from the inside out.

Lesson XX: Honesty Over Convenience

Convenience is persuasive and smooths edges, while avoiding tension and promising ease. Honesty slows the moment, introduces friction where shortcuts once lived, and requires standing still long enough to feel what is true, even when truth complicates the path forward. Many choose convenience without realizing the cost.

A small omission here, softened truth there, and silence where clarity was needed are choices that accumulate quietly. Integrity erodes through accommodation more than betrayal. Over time, the inner compass weakens, confusion replaces confidence, and fatigue settles where clarity once lived. The body notices immediately.

Truth begins internally, long before being spoken aloud. Jiddu Krishnamurti insisted that *"Being truthful to oneself is the highest form of intelligence."* Convenience often enters as self-betrayal before appearing in speech. When inner honesty is compromised, perception distorts and choice narrows. Clarity returns through willingness to see what is happening without justification or escape. This seeing reorganizes action naturally.

When honesty is withheld, tension forms. The breath then shortens, nervous system braces, and energy drains while managing what must be remembered, avoided, or defended. Honesty restores coherence. When truth is spoken cleanly, the body relaxes and alignment returns.

Language, too, reflects the moral consequences of convenience. George Orwell warned that *"The great enemy of clear language is insincerity."* When words are chosen to obscure rather than reveal, thought follows suit. Honesty sharpens language, and sharpened language clarifies thought. This clarity restores orientation. One knows where one stands, even when the ground is uneven.

Even when consequences follow, relief arrives alongside them and the burden of maintenance dissolves. Honesty is precision that does not require excess explanation or demand performance. Honesty simply states what is real and allows life to respond accordingly.

Convenience seeks comfort now while honesty protects wholeness later. This principle applies inward as much as outward. Self-deception fractures trust and rationalization delays growth. Facing reality through habit, pattern, and desire opens the door to change. Truth spoken internally reorganizes behavior naturally.

History shows that collective harm often begins with small personal evasions. Aleksandr Solzhenitsyn traced this pattern precisely, writing, *"Live not by lies."* This instruction is not heroic rhetoric but daily discipline. Each time truth is softened for ease, a subtle fracture forms. Over time, these fractures accumulate until reality feels unstable. Honesty restores solidity by removing the need to manage falsehood.

Honesty may cost approval, disrupt familiarity, or require courage, yet pays in freedom. When honesty becomes habit, life simplifies, decisions clarify, relationships stabilize, direction sharpens, and integrity endures.

Existential thinkers recognized that truth is often uncomfortable precisely because of a demand for responsibility. Søren Kierkegaard wrote, *"The most common form of despair is not being who you are."* Convenience offers temporary relief from this despair by allowing one to perform rather than inhabit life. Honesty ends the performance. While this may cost ease, freedom is returned. To live honestly is to stand in alignment with what is real, and to let life respond without distortion.

Remember that authenticity is the highest frequency and being honest with yourself is being authentic to your radiance. You only fool yourself when your actions and intentions are dishonest.

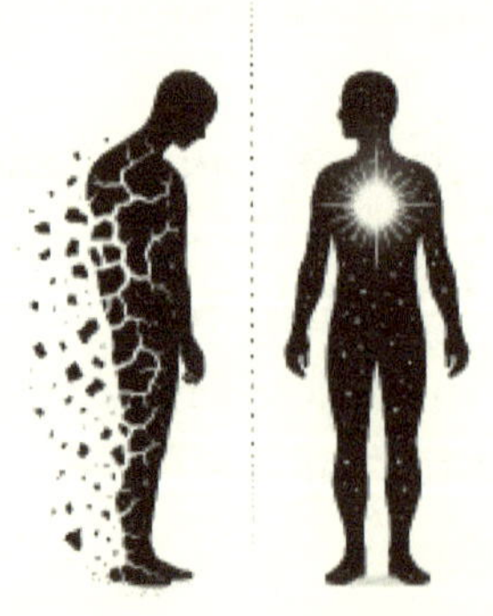

Lesson XXI: Show Up for What Matters

My children live in different states, with different mothers, and time together is limited to one week each month during the school schedule. There is no flexibility in that window. I travel to them without exception. Weather, fatigue, cost, or complication do not alter the commitment.

My presence is not outsourced, delayed, or replaced with explanation. Antoine de Saint-Exupéry captured this responsibility simply: *"Love does not consist in gazing at each other, but in looking outward together in the same direction."* Showing up teaches children something no words can convey that they are worth crossing distance for, every time.

Clarity means little without presence and intention dissolves without participation. Life reveals priorities through attendance. What matters receives time, energy, and consistency, even when conditions are imperfect. Showing up looks like returning when enthusiasm fades, staying when convenience invites departure, and tending small responsibilities long before recognition appears.

Consistency communicates safety more clearly than affection alone. Children do not measure love by intensity, but by arrival. Viktor Schauberger observed that *"Nature understands no jesting; she is always true, always serious, and always severe. She is always right."* Life follows the same law. What is tended flourishes and what is postponed weakens.

When a parent arrives reliably, the nervous system of the child settles into trust. The message is embodied that they matter enough to be chosen repeatedly.

Khalil Gibran wrote, *"Work is love made visible."* Presence is love made tangible and this requires willingness. What matters most in life asks for the courage to arrive when absence would be easier. Legacy is formed by where we consistently place our body, our time, and our attention. I endure staggering travel expenses and consistently miss work as an exchange for spending quality time with my kids. Staying home would be a lot easier, but this would be inauthentic and cost me more morally.

Many wait to feel ready, for certainty, and for motivation to arrive before committing attention, yet what matters most often asks for presence before confidence follows. Showing up creates momentum. When effort is offered regularly, connection deepens, relationships stabilize, skills mature, purpose clarifies, and life begins to organize around what is reliably honored.

Avoidance fragments meaning but consistency restores. To show up means offering oneself fully to the moment at hand. This is demonstrated by listening carefully, acting honestly, and remaining engaged even when results lag effort. What matters rarely demands perfection but asks for sincerity. When showing up becomes habit, discipline softens into devotion, and action feels less like obligation and more like alignment. The body recognizes reliability and responds with steadiness. Life notices this too.

Showing up is a physical act repeated over time. Seneca understood this plainly when he wrote, *"He who is brave is free."* Bravery, here, is the willingness to remain present when logistics are difficult and comfort is unavailable. To show up consistently requires freedom from excuses and negotiation. This is the choice to let responsibility outweigh convenience until reliability becomes character.

Paths open for those who arrive repeatedly, opportunities emerge for those who demonstrate commitment through presence rather than proclamation, and trust accumulates quietly. Showing up is a form of respect toward others, toward purpose, and toward the self that is becoming through repetition. In the end, what matters is shaped by who was willing to remain present when leaving would have been easier.

Lesson XXII: The Reciprocity Is in the Giving

Character is proven where reward is not guaranteed and legacy is forged where recognition does not always follow. Both are revealed in the unguarded moments when no exchange is expected, no advantage is gained, and generosity meets silence. How we treat those who cannot repay us tells the truth about who we are.

Ancient wisdom understood how one treats the powerless reveals alignment with natural law. Laozi taught, *"Kindness in words creates confidence. Kindness in thinking creates profoundness. Kindness in giving creates love."* Kindness offered without expectation refines strength and signals inner sufficiency. This is the knowledge that nothing needs to be extracted from another to feel whole.

Power tempts performance and influence invites calculation, yet the soul is shaped in kindness offered without witnesses, patience extended without return, and care given where nothing comes back. Children notice this, animals feel this, and the vulnerable remember. These encounters leave marks deeper than achievements.

The discipline of compassion without transaction has always stood apart from sentimentality. Simone Weil described attention as a moral act, writing, *"Attention is the rarest and purest form of generosity."* To truly attend to another person, especially one without power, influence, or utility, requires restraint of self-interest.

This form of generosity does not perform goodness but practices presence. Legacy is built from these quiet acts of seeing. When nothing is owed, choice becomes pure. Kindness offered without calculation settles somewhere unseen and softens the world incrementally. This goodness restores faith quietly and moves forward through lives never met again. When you offer gifts, do not expect anything back.

As Khalil Gibran so simply expressed, *"It is when you give of yourself that you truly give."* This giving cannot be audited or repaid because this is an expression of being. What remains after titles fade and accomplishments dissolve is the way dignity was extended, especially to those who had nothing to offer in return. This is how character becomes legacy. The reciprocity is in the giving.

When help is offered freely, integrity strengthens. When compassion is selective, character fractures quietly. The difference is not always visible, but life records everything. The way one speaks to service workers, responds to inconvenience, and treats those without leverage shapes legacy. To give without expectation is sovereignty expressed as trust. These gestures exude confidence that worth does not require validation. This is the understanding that generosity refines the giver.

No monument captures this, and no metric measures this, yet life remembers. Character grows when compassion is extended beyond fairness and legacy endures when dignity is honored universally. In the end, what remains is not what was accumulated, but what was embodied, especially when no one was watching.

True character is revealed most clearly where there is no audience and no advantage. Epictetus articulated this with uncompromising honesty: *"If you want to improve, be content to be thought foolish and stupid."* To treat those who cannot repay us with respect often costs comfort, efficiency, or pride. The ego resists such moments because no status is gained, yet integrity strengthens precisely where the ego finds no reward.

There were many instances in my life when people in my community reached out to help me get through challenging circumstances. I reciprocated this later in life every way I could. This keeps the flow going.

Lesson XXIII: Live Compassionately in an Unconscious World

To see clearly in a world moving quickly, distracted by noise and urgency, is not always comfortable. Compassion becomes a practice rather than an instinct when surroundings reward indifference, speed, and self-protection. I learned that compassion is when we feel the pain and suffering of every living being.

Compassion begins with perception rather than reaction. Thích Quảng Đức is remembered not only for protest, but for clarity under unbearable conditions, reminding the world that *"Compassion is the most important thing in life."* This compassion was moral gravity. In an unconscious world, compassion often means slowing the impulse to judge and choosing to see what is operating beneath behavior. This seeing does not excuse harm but prevents the heart from hardening in response.

An unconscious world means a world forgetting how actions ripple, words land, and how every person carries unseen history. To live compassionately within such conditions requires restraint and asks for patience when reaction would be easier. This requires understanding when judgment feels justified and asks for softness without surrendering clarity.

Compassion is strength held gently. To carry compassion means choosing not to mirror harm, even when harm is encountered, refusing to let bitterness define perception, and remembering that behavior often masks pain rather than intention.

Living this way can feel lonely. Those who move consciously are often misunderstood. Their sensitivity is sometimes mistaken for weakness and boundaries are seen as distance. Compassion, however, remains steady, because integrity demands consistency.

Modern contemplative teachers emphasize that compassion must be paired with steadiness to endure. Pema Chödrön writes, *"Compassion becomes real when we recognize our shared humanity."* In an unconscious world, this recognition means acknowledging the common roots of fear, confusion, and longing beneath behavior. Compassion then becomes spacious and allows one to respond without being consumed, remain open without being eroded, and offer kindness without losing center.

To live compassionately in an unconscious world is to offer light without insisting on recognition, move through confusion without contributing, and remain human where numbness is normalized. Every act of compassion interrupts a pattern, each moment of patience restores coherence, and a refusal to harden keeps the heart available.

Compassion in an unconscious world begins with the refusal to let reactivity dictate response. The Buddhist philosopher Shantideva wrote with striking precision, *"All the happiness there is in this world arises from wishing others to be happy."* This is strategic intelligence.

Compassion redirects energy away from resentment and toward coherence. In a world driven by impulse, to choose compassion is to interrupt reflex and remain oriented toward what preserves life rather than what multiplies harm.

This path requires discernment. Not every action requires engagement or conflict deserves energy. Wounds do not have to be reopened. Compassion includes oneself. To remain awake without burning out, care must be replenished.

Silence restores balance, nature recalibrates perspective, and breath returns the body to center. Compassion without self-respect becomes depletion. A conscious heart learns to witness without absorbing. This is your invitation to practice compassion.

Lesson XXIV: Release Others from the Debt of Your Pain

Pain keeps accounts. Memories replay and stories sharpen while the mind rehearses what was taken, what was unfair, and what should have been different. In this accounting, energy remains tethered to the past. The one who caused harm continues to occupy space after departure.

Punishment promises relief and rarely delivers freedom. Holding another in debt binds the nervous system to injury. Anger stays vigilant and the body remains braced. Time moves forward, yet the moment of pain repeats internally. Release changes this equation.

Ancient wisdom recognized that punishment binds the sufferer as tightly as the offender. Aeschylus observed, *"He who learns must suffer."* The deeper lesson, however, is not suffering but how one responds. When pain is carried forward as grievance, suffering multiplies. If metabolized into understanding, suffering completes a purpose. Release is the decision to extract wisdom without continuing the wound.

To release another from the debt of pain is to end the transaction, reclaim energy trapped in vigilance, and refuse further payment from one's own life. Forgiveness is often misunderstood as softness. In truth, forgiveness is precision that cuts the cord cleanly and returns authorship to the present. Punishment keeps the wound active while release allows repair to begin.

This does not require reconciliation, or demand forgetting, but asks only for willingness to stop feeding the injury. Our body recognizes release immediately. Breath deepens, muscles loosen, and sleep returns in depth. What punishment could never offer, which is primarily peace, arrives quietly.

Release restores movement. The future then regains possibility, identity separates from harm, and life resumes forward motion without dragging the past behind. This freedom grows through compassion, not obligation, cannot be forced, and arrives when readiness meets understanding.

I am writing of compassion for the self who endured, the humanity that faltered, and the truth that carrying pain longer will not undo the experience. To release is to choose life over rehearsal, trust healing more than justice alone, and step back into authorship. Freedom expands when the past is no longer owed anything. In this freedom, the soul breathes again.

Contemplative traditions emphasize that inner freedom is never achieved through external judgment alone. James Allen wrote, *"A man is the product of his thoughts; what he thinks, he becomes."* When thoughts remain tethered to past harm, identity contracts around injury. When release is chosen, thought reorganizes, energy returns to the present, and authorship is restored. Forgiveness, in this sense, is not absolution of another, but reclamation of the self.

Blame is understood as a burden that restricts movement. Alfred Adler taught that *"It is easier to fight for one's principles than to live up to them."* Living up to release requires courage and asks the injured party to relinquish the false power of resentment in exchange for the real power of mobility. When blame is released, the psyche regains flexibility and future reopens.

I was betrayed many times in my life and specifically by someone who I loved wholeheartedly. Carrying resentment or low vibrational energy associated with this person would never resolve the past, so I diffused everything bad that happened and decided to only remember the quality moments we shared. I adjusted to become a better person as well and accepted accountability for the role I played.

Lesson XXV: Get Familiar With the Sacred

The sacred is revealed to those who stay. Convictions spoken are easy, while those that are lived are costly. To stand for something invites friction, living by truth attracts resistance, and refusing compromise welcomes consequence. This is where belief becomes embodied.

Poets, too, have always known that truth must be suffered before spoken with authority. William Blake wrote, *"No bird soars too high if he soars with his own wings."* To soar with one's own wings is to risk falling without excuse. Conviction becomes sacred when belief is no longer borrowed, inherited, or convenient, but carried through consequence. This self-bearing is the mark of initiation.

Bleeding is not always literal. Often, bleeding arrives as loss of comfort, approval, or certainty. Relationships strain, paths narrow, and old identities dissolve. Something must be surrendered for integrity to remain intact. The sacred recognizes this exchange.

What is not tested remains theoretical. What is tested becomes truth carried in the body. Conviction matures when pressure is survived. Wisdom deepens when ideals are chosen despite inconvenience. Those who have never paid a price for their values often confuse preference with principle. When conditions shift, preference collapses and principle remains. Bleeding refines intention.

Indigenous wisdom carries this understanding without abstraction. Chief Seattle spoke from a place of lived relationship when he said, *"All things are connected. Whatever befalls the Earth befalls the children of the Earth."* This awareness is not conceptual but earned through experiences that dissolve separation and restore humility. Conviction tested by hardship softens the illusion of individuality and returns us to participation within something greater than the self. The sacred opens where surrender replaces certainty.

Not everyone is called to walk this path or desires these demands, yet those who do find something unshakeable. Conviction that has been tested moves quietly, stands without argument, and radiates stability rather than force. To bleed for conviction is to allow life to shape belief into bone. Once that shaping occurs, the sacred is known intimately through scars, courage, and continued presence.

Those who have walked the path of conviction consistently warn that truth is revealed only under pressure. Friedrich Nietzsche wrote, *"Only great pain is the ultimate liberator of the spirit."* Pain, here, is not glorified, but acknowledged as clarifying. When comfort dissolves, illusions fall away, and what remains is what one is truly willing to stand for. The sacred is not announced in ease but appears when the will is stripped of ornament and forced into honesty.

Aleksandr Solzhenitsyn observed, *"One word of truth outweighs the whole world."* A word of truth spoken without cost, however, is easily dismissed. Truth gains gravity when lived despite loss. The sacred recognizes weight, not volume. Conviction that has bled no longer needs defense but stands because of surviving.

I learned over the years that when something is defended through sacrifice, this moves beyond concept and becomes orientation. The nervous system then aligns, body commits, and soul recognizes coherence. This is why sacred knowledge cannot be rushed. Initiation arrives through endurance, meaning clarifies through lived consequence, and the sacred opens only when devotion proves sincere.

What is sacred is allured by frequency, harmony, and authenticity. To attract more sacredness in your life, start by shifting your perspective and recognizing the sacredness in all life. This mindfulness goes a long way.

Lesson XXVI: We Can Omit Chapters From Our Story

A story ends after being integrated. Life unfolds in chapters. Some are formative, while others are necessary, and few are painful teachers that arrive without invitation. No chapter, however, is required to remain active forever. Authorship includes editing.

Ancient philosophy recognized this law of movement long before psychology claimed labels. Heraclitus taught that *"No man ever steps in the same river twice."* The self is already changing, whether permission is granted or not. To cling to an outdated chapter is to resist a reality already in motion. Omission is not rejection of truth, but alignment with flux. What is released makes room for the present to be met without distortion.

To omit a chapter is to release authority over the present. We are not denying that these experiences happened, we are simply minimizing how they impact our present. The past does not disappear, but the role changes. What once defined identity becomes material for growth.

Composting is transformation. Old stories of failure, shame, addiction, or survival carry nutrients. When held with awareness, they enrich the soil of wisdom. When clung to unconsciously, they restrict growth. The difference lies in intention. What is composted nourishes the future.

Pain teaches discernment, loss emphasizes value, and mistakes highlight humility, yet when these lessons are extracted, the story no longer needs repetition. The work is then complete. Many remain loyal to outdated narratives out of familiarity. Identity calcifies around who one was rather than who one is becoming. Freedom returns when allegiance shifts from history to possibility. The body understands this instinctively.

Digestion extracts what nourishes and releases what does not. The psyche follows the same law. Experience enters, meaning is gathered, and the rest must pass through. Healing accelerates when stories soften. The nervous system relaxes, energy unbinds, creativity returns, and the future regains elasticity.

Writers have long understood that identity is not fixed by what has occurred but shaped by what is carried forward. Anaïs Nin captured this freedom succinctly: *"We write to taste life twice, in the moment and in retrospect."* Retrospect is meant for understanding, not for permanent residence.

Once meaning has been extracted, the work of the chapter has been completed. To continue living inside the story is to mistake reflection for reality. Authorship matures when one knows when to close the book and begin again.

To compost the old story is to honor without living inside, to carry forward wisdom rather than wound, and to let the soil of experience feed new growth.

You are not required to reread every chapter, or are you obligated to relive every scene. You have permission to turn the page deliberately. What remains becomes medicine, while what is released becomes space. In this space, a new chapter begins that is rooted in truth, nourished by experience, and open to light.

Depth psychology later echoed this necessity of renewal through integration rather than fixation. D.W. Winnicott observed that *"It is a joy to be hidden and a disaster not to be found."* When old stories dominate identity, the living self remains concealed beneath repetition.

Omitting a chapter allows the true self to surface no longer defined by survival alone, but free to create, relate, and imagine. Healing accelerates when the psyche is allowed to reorganize around who one is now, rather than who one had to be.

Lesson XXVII: Mistakes Are the Soil of Transformation

Mistakes are often considered evidence of failure and treated as something to correct quickly, hide, or move past without looking back. Nothing, however, grows without disturbance. Soil becomes fertile only after being broken open. Roots do not deepen in untouched ground.

Transformation requires contact, or friction between intention and reality, and what was hoped for and what occurred. Mistakes reveal where attention was absent. They expose where care was needed and mark the places where love had not yet learned how to arrive. To make a mistake is not to lack worth but to encounter a boundary of understanding.

What matters is what follows. When mistakes are met with punishment, growth contracts, shame hardens the soil, and the lesson remains inaccessible. When mistakes are met with curiosity and compassion, the ground softens, insight enters, and love finds a place to root. This is how maturity forms. A mistake says *something here wants care,* then points toward an unmet need and highlights a place where presence was missing.

Transformation asks for willingness to look closely, feel responsibility without self-rejection, and stay with the lesson until wisdom emerges. The body understands this process instinctively.

Injury heals stronger when supported, scar tissue forms where protection is required, and life reinforces where attention has been earned.

Love grows roots where mistakes once lived. What was once fragile becomes resilient and what collapsed eventually becomes stable. The place that failed becomes the place that holds. Mistakes compost into understanding when met honestly. They become teachers rather than verdicts. They shape character gently when allowed to do their work.

I write this as someone who has made real mistakes, not abstract ones. Decisions I made cost me my freedom on more than one occasion. Consequences arrived fully and without negotiation. There were moments when the ground gave way beneath me and I had no choice but to sit with what I had done, what I had avoided, and what I had misunderstood. Those periods stripped away excuses and illusions. What remained was the opportunity to learn.

Each time I was forced to stop, I paid attention. I studied my patterns, examined the beliefs that led me there, and noticed where impulse replaced discernment and where unhealed pain was driving behavior. Adjustment followed awareness. I changed how I lived, how I chose, how I related to authority, and how I listened to consequence.

Growth did not come from punishment, but from what I extracted while enduring. Freedom returned only when change became embodied rather than promised.

Confucius taught, *"When we see men of a contrary character, we should turn inwards and examine ourselves."* Mistakes that turn attention inward become teachers and mistakes that are met only with shame repeat. What altered my life was not avoiding error afterward but learning how to metabolize error into insight and redirect energy toward something more coherent.

I no longer see mistakes as evidence of deficiency. I see them as markers along a path that required correction. They refined my values, sharpened my discernment, and clarified what kind of man I was willing to become.

Each misstep asked for a deeper level of responsibility and every consequence demanded a better version of myself. Transformation did not happen despite those mistakes but because I stayed with the lesson long enough.

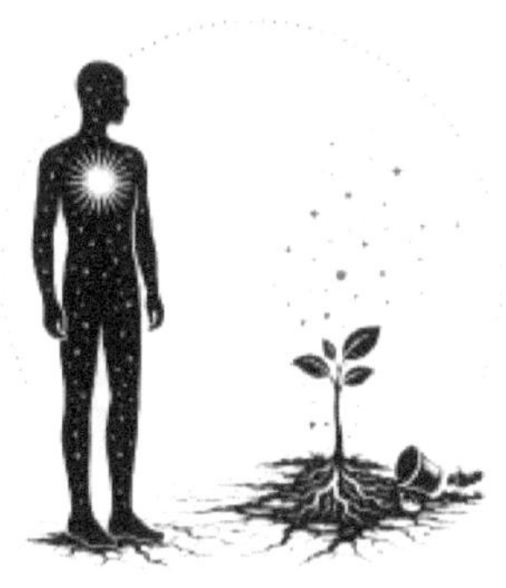

Lesson XXVIII: Dancing with Difficulty

At first, difficulty feels like something to fix, or outrun, that is standing in the way of the life that was supposed to happen. Much of early living is spent resisting what arises. We push against pain, argue with circumstance, and wait for conditions to improve before allowing presence to arrive.

A moment comes, often after exhaustion, when resistance loosens, escape no longer satisfies, avoidance grows heavy, and running circles back to the same place. In this moment, something shifts. Rather than bracing against difficulty, attention turns toward the challenges. Our body softens, breath steadies, and curiosity replaces urgency. Difficulty is no longer treated as an enemy, but as a partner. This is where the dance begins.

I learned this dance as life required me to. Loss arrived early for me and without permission. The death of my father and the suicide of my brother were not events to resolve, but realities to live inside. There was no clean exit from grief and no shortcut around pain.

What carried me forward was learning how to stay in motion without denying sorrow. As Khalil Gibran wrote, *"The deeper that sorrow carves into your being, the more joy you can contain."* Grief, when met rather than avoided, reshapes the inner architecture and widens capacity rather than collapsing.

Dancing with difficulty means moving with what is present rather than freezing or fleeing, adapting rhythm instead of demanding silence, and allowing life to lead without surrendering agency. Acceptance arrives quietly, not as defeat, but alignment. When difficulty is met with acceptance, energy previously spent resisting becomes available for intelligence. Solutions then emerge organically, strength redistributes, and the nervous system exits survival and reenters participation. Grace is revealed here.

Grace is not the removal of hardship but the capacity to remain open within. Movement becomes possible again, humor returns, and perspective widens when the body discovers that difficulty, when met honestly, acts as an instructor. Acceptance teaches timing, humility, and trust. This grace feels like steadiness, balance regained, and standing upright in imperfect conditions.

Over time, I discovered that grace is not something granted after pain passes, but what is cultivated while pain remains present. Pema Chödrön wrote, *"Only to the extent that we expose ourselves over and over to annihilation can that which is indestructible in us be found."*

Difficulty reveals what endures. By staying present, adjusting pace, and refusing to abandon myself in the face of loss, I learned that strength is not forged through escape, but through participation. The dance continues because movement is a way of life.

To dance with difficulty is to acknowledge reality without surrendering faith, move forward without demanding certainty, and participate fully even if the music is unfamiliar. This is the grace of acceptance, not passive or resigned, but alive. Once this is known, escape loses appeal.

There were seasons in my life when standing felt unbearable, yet running offered no relief. Movement became medicine as dialogue with what hurt. Friedrich Nietzsche captured this truth plainly: *"One must still have chaos in oneself to be able to give birth to a dancing star."* Dancing with difficulty does not eliminate chaos but teaches how to move within without being consumed. Rhythm returns where rigidity once lived and balance is found by responsiveness.

When experiencing challenging circumstances, the four solutions you can count on are hydrating your cells and organs with pure water, moving your body in nature, being exposed to direct sunlight, and breathing mindfully.

Lesson XXIX: Change Your Prayer to Improve Conditions

Prayer is alignment. I learned over many moons that Spirit responds to posture, certainty, and coherence. What is spoken carries weight only when the body stands behind the words. Many prayers fail because they are uninhabited. A prayer whispered from collapse communicates doubt, and one spoken while slouched signals uncertainty. A prayer that contradicts belief dissolves before reaching action.

Buddhist wisdom also cautions against spiritual posturing divorced from embodiment. Chögyam Trungpa taught, *"The essence of warriorship is fearlessness, the willingness to step out of hope and fear."* Prayer grounded in fear hopes for rescue, while prayer grounded in presence stands firm. Declaration is steadiness and the refusal to bargain with uncertainty and the decision to meet life upright.

Modern contemplative teachers emphasize that prayer works through frequency rather than force. Richard Rudd describes this as coherence, noting that *"The frequency you hold determines the reality you experience."* Prayer that emerges from fear reinforces contraction, while prayer that arises from trust broadcasts stability. When inner tone shifts, the outer world responds differently.

To change conditions, prayer must mature into declaration. This means authority without strain. We pray with an upright spine, steady breath, and words spoken as truth rather than request. Prayer becomes command, not demanding from life, but declaring alignment.

"I choose clarity." "I act with integrity." "I trust the unfolding." "I affirm prosperity." These are orientations and declarations, not wishes. When prayer is embodied, the nervous system stabilizes and thought organizes. Action follows naturally and life responds to the signal being broadcast. Belief is congruence, not volume.

Early metaphysical teachers understood that prayer is not a request sent outward, but a state assumed inward. Florence Scovel Shinn wrote, *"Your word is your wand."* Words spoken without embodiment lack direction, but words spoken from certainty reorganize circumstance. Prayer, in this sense, is not asking life to change, but aligning oneself so that change becomes unavoidable. When speech, belief, and posture agree, prayer acquires leverage.

The body must agree with the words, breath must support the voice, and mind must not quietly argue while the mouth speaks affirmation. When belief is present, prayer stops sounding desperate and begins sounding inevitable. This is why posture and presence matters, and why truth must be spoken only when lived.

Contemporary neuroscience now echoes what mystics long observed. Joe Dispenza explains, *"When you combine a clear intention with an elevated emotion, you begin to change your biology."* Prayer alters conditions by adjusting the nervous system. When the body believes what the mind declares, chemistry shifts, perception reorganizes, and behavior aligns. Conditions then follow biology. Change the prayer, and the body learns how to live as if the answer has already arrived.

I learned throughout my life that changing my prayer improves my conditions in life and the quality of my experiences. I went from pleading to standing, hoping to choosing, and asking to embodying. My prayers are embodied with belief, confidence, and declaration. In my younger years, they were clouded by circumstance, doubt, and partial faith.

Life mirrors clarity and reflects certainty. Change the prayer, not in language alone, but in your stance, breath, posture, and belief. When prayer becomes declaration, conditions follow.

Lesson XXX: Intention Is A Vow

A vow commits from within. My friends and I omitted the words wish and hope from our vocabulary many years ago and replaced them with the word trust. To wish for something is not an affirmation. To trust is to affirm. Rather than suggesting, *"I hope for a miracle,"* the reframing for this statement is the declaration, *"I trust all that I require is coming my way."*

Mystics understood that vow alters destiny by altering direction. Rabindranath Tagore observed, *"Faith is the bird that feels the light and sings when the dawn is still dark."* A vow is this kind of faith. I am not referencing blind optimism, but steady participation before evidence appears. Trust precedes visibility. When intention becomes vow, action begins before confirmation, and the future reorganizes around that steadiness.

A vow holds steady when conditions fluctuate and does not negotiate with comfort. Our focus remains present when motivation wanes and does not wait for permission from circumstance. This is why intention must be chosen carefully. Every vow enters the bloodstream of daily life, shaping habits quietly, informing response, and determining what is tolerated and what is released.

Intention is often spoken lightly, as if naming a desire alone will summon the manifestation and fulfillment of what we are calling in. True intention carries weight, alters posture, reorganizes behavior, and demands consistency long after enthusiasm fades.

A vow changes the nervous system. When intention becomes vow, the body aligns, choices simplify, and distractions lose authority. Energy gathers around direction rather than dispersing across possibility.

Modern contemplative teachers describe vow as a frequency of alignment rather than ambition. Thich Nhat Hanh wrote, *"With mindfulness, concentration, and insight, we can realize our true home."* A vow stabilizes the mind and concentrates energy. Distraction weakens when devotion strengthens. When one lives from vow rather than wish, the nervous system settles into coherence and choice becomes less scattered.

A vow is reliable. When intention is embodied as vow, integrity becomes effortless. Action then follows naturally and the gap between belief and behavior closes. Life responds to this coherence as opportunities align, resistance clarifies, and support emerges from unexpected places.

A wish asks, *"Will this happen?"*, and a vow declares, *"This is happening."* The vow guarantees participation and accepts responsibility for the path ahead while standing upright inside uncertainty.

Even contemporary thinkers speak of intention as embodied commitment rather than mental projection. Wayne Dyer wrote, *"When you change the way you look at things, the things you look at change."* A vow shifts perception first. When perception shifts, behavior follows, and conditions then respond.

Intention declared lightly evaporates, but intention sealed as vow rewires identity, and when lived consistently this reshapes circumstance.

When intention is sealed as vow, trust deepens, because alignment is intact. Intention becomes destiny through devotion expressed daily. I learned with time to choose vows wisely, then live them patiently, and let life respond in time.

Lesson XXXI: Illness Is a Messenger

Our body speaks when listening has been postponed. Childhood conditioning directs us to ignore the messages that are telling us what we are eating and how we are living is depleting us. Illness emerges when patterns persist beyond tolerance, pace overrides rhythm, values drift from action, and nourishment gives way to compensation. Symptoms then arise as a form of communication.

Early natural hygienists spoke clearly about illness as consequence rather than catastrophe. Hilton Hotema taught, *"Disease is the result of the violation of Nature's laws."* When the body falls ill, this is signaling deviation from biological harmony. Hotema emphasized that vitality returns when the body is relieved of burden and restored to foods that carry light, order, and mineral intelligence rather than decay.

The body speaks in sensation because sensation cannot be ignored. Fatigue slows what speed has disrupted and pain interrupts what has been overextended. Inflammation highlights where boundaries have been crossed physically, emotionally, or spiritually. Illness calls our attention back.

Often, illness arrives after subtler signals were dismissed. Whispers become discomfort, which is then experienced through dysfunction. Our body escalates the language until alignment is addressed. To listen is the first act of healing. Listening means asking honestly: *What has fallen out of harmony? What is being asked to change? What truth has been postponed?*

When nourishment returns, vitality stirs. As rest is honored, repair begins. If integrity is reclaimed, energy reorganizes. Healing unfolds when life is met honestly rather than managed aggressively. Force rarely restores balance and understanding often does.

Natural hygiene pioneers consistently emphasized that vitality is restored through alignment with nature's original design. Herbert Shelton wrote, *"Health is normal. Disease is abnormal."* Illness, then, is not an enemy to defeat but a signal to correct course. Shelton taught that when the body is returned to living foods, clean water, sunlight, rest, and emotional integrity, healing becomes inevitable rather than forced. The body already knows how to regenerate. Alignment simply removes the interference.

Illness becomes a teacher. Through illness, priorities clarify, illusions dissolve, and the soul is invited back into the body as a guide. When alignment is restored, symptoms soften, energy redistributes, and our body resumes the quiet work of regeneration.

Even when complete recovery is not immediate, our relationship with faith is adjusted, and this change carries power. The body seeks balance and our soul remembers the way. Illness asks for attention, healing requires honesty, and alignment restores dialogue. Once there is congruence, the healing process starts from within.

Pioneers of living nutrition recognized that the body heals most effectively when given life rather than stimulation. Ann Wigmore wrote, *"The food you eat can be either the safest and most powerful form of medicine, or the slowest form of poison."*

Living foods speak directly to cellular intelligence. They reduce inflammation by restoring communication. When illness arises, Wigmore taught that the question is not what drug is missing, but what life force has been excluded.

I learned from life experience that if we are sick, feeling unwell, or simply uncomfortable, this is a messenger encouraging us to adjust our lifestyle and trust the redirected path in front of us.

Lesson XXXII: Live in Such a Way That the Earth Is Grateful for Your Footprints

The Earth remembers how we walk. Every step leaves more than an impression on soil. We imprint our intentions, tonality, and relationship. The land responds to how presence is carried across the terrain. To live in a way that honors the Earth is about reciprocity.

Indigenous earth-based teachers remind us that the land is living intelligence. Arkan Lushwala, in *The Time of the Black Jaguar*, writes that *"The Earth is not a resource; she is a being with her own consciousness and destiny."* To walk in a way that the Earth would be grateful is to recognize her as participant, not property.

When soil is treated as relative rather than commodity, behavior changes. Reverence then replaces entitlement, listening overrides extraction, and footprints become conversation rather than intrusion.

Gratitude expressed through behavior speaks louder than any declaration. When choices reduce harm, rhythms respect regeneration, and consumption considers consequence, the Earth responds with resilience.

The angelic realms notice the way we live and keep track of how water is treated, food is chosen, waste is handled, and silence is respected. Small decisions accumulate into impact. The Earth and all our guiding forces appreciate our awareness.

Ecological thinkers have long reminded us that the Earth is not resource, but relationship. Vandana Shiva writes, *"In nature's economy, the currency is not money but is life."* When we forget this, we reduce the living world to transaction. To live in such a way that the Earth would be grateful for our footprints is to return to life as currency with soil replenished, water protected, seeds saved, and diversity honored. Our choices should nourish rather than extract.

To walk lightly is to recognize interdependence. To move deliberately is to understand life through balance. When integrity governs action, even footprints become blessing. Living this way restores humility.

Human life is part of a larger organism. Breath exchanges with trees, soil feeds bodies, and water circulates endlessly. Everything participates in a distinct way, and no action exists in isolation. When alignment returns, stewardship follows naturally. Care soon replaces exploitation, while listening overrules dominance, and presence takes the place of entitlement.

Anthropologist Wade Davis echoes this relational understanding, writing, *"The world into which you are born does not exist in some absolute sense but is just one model of reality."* Many cultures have lived with cosmologies in which mountains are ancestors, rivers are teachers, and forests are kin.

To live gratefully upon the Earth is to remember that our modern model is not the only way of seeing. Our perception must shift from dominion to reciprocity.

The Earth responds generously to respect, regeneration accelerates when pressure softens, and abundance returns when balance is restored. This is an example of a sacred way of relating with the cosmic intelligence permeating around.

To live gratefully is to move with consideration. We must recognize that progress without reverence fractures the future. We start to understand that sustainability is not restraint, but wisdom applied over time.

My invitation for you is to allow the land to feel safe beneath your steps, let water move cleanly because of your choices, and be a reason why future generations inherit ground that still knows how to give.

I learned over the years when our footprints carry integrity, the Earth answers quietly with nourishment, protection, and stability.

Lesson XXXIII: Be the Kind of Person Someone Will Write A Poem About

Poems are often written about presence. They arise from moments that linger such as an unexpected kindness, quiet courage, or way of listening that makes another feel seen. Poetry remembers what efficiency forgets. To live poetically is to move through the world with care.

Poetry has always emerged from attention paid to the ordinary. Rainer Maria Rilke understood this intimately, writing, *"Try to learn to love what is simple."* The poetic life is shaped through devotion to small acts done with care. A life becomes worthy of poetry when lived with enough presence that nothing is rushed past or treated as insignificant.

The kind of person someone writes a poem about is not the loudest in the room or even the most accomplished or most admired. That person is remembered for how life felt nearby. Gentleness leaves an imprint, integrity creates rhythm, and humor softens gravity.

Poems are born from gestures that expect nothing in return. This could be from patience offered when frustration would be easier, dignity maintained when compromise beckons, or love expressed without strategy. This is an art practiced daily.

The quality that lingers most in memory is not brilliance, but kindness carried with consistency. Maya Angelou captured this truth simply: *"People will never forget how you made them feel."*

Feeling is the medium of poetry. When someone leaves another person feeling steadied, respected, or quietly uplifted, something lasting has been written into the fabric of experience. This is how influence travels without announcement.

How one speaks to strangers, holds silence, and treats the overlooked are details that compose character. A poetic life seeks resonance over applause and understands that meaning travels through subtlety, influence moves quietly, and the most enduring impressions are felt rather than announced. Kindness becomes atmosphere when consistent.

Across cultures, wisdom traditions agree that beauty arises from how one inhabits the world. Rabindranath Tagore wrote, *"Let your life lightly dance on the edges of Time like dew on the tip of a leaf."* A poetic life moves with grace, leaving freshness rather than weight behind. Such a person becomes a memory others carry gently, long after words have fallen away.

Poetic lives also know how to make space. Leonard Cohen wrote, *"There is a crack in everything. That is how the light gets in."* To live poetically is to allow honesty, vulnerability, and humility to soften the edges of self. These openings create intimacy and invite others to breathe more easily and feel less alone in their own imperfections.

Honesty becomes trust when embodied and compassion can feel like refuge when activated. This is how poetry enters the world, through living examples. Long after words are forgotten, tone remains. When achievements fade, presence echoes. People remember how they felt in the company of those who lived with care.

I encourage you to be that memory and let your life speak gently. Allow for your actions to rhyme with your values and your presence to leave the world more human than when you arrived. That is the poem worth writing.

Lesson XXXIV: There Is No Retirement for the Soul

The soul does not measure life in milestones or recognize finish lines. Only the mind imagines a day when becoming ends, effort ceases, curiosity rests, and contribution is no longer required. The soul continues quietly, asking to express, serve, and refine.

Some of the clearest wisdom about lifelong purpose comes from those who understood time as a deepening rather than a decline. Rabindranath Tagore wrote, *"Age considers; youth ventures."* The soul does not stop venturing, though the ventures become subtler.

Later life is not meant for withdrawal, but for discernment, and seeing more clearly what matters and offering that clarity to the world. What once required force matures into guidance. What sought achievement ripens into understanding. The soul continues the work through refinement.

Purpose does not expire. Bodies slow, roles change, and seasons turn, yet the inner call remains active, adapting voice to circumstance. What once required force may later require presence. What demanded labor may eventually ask for guidance. Expression matures rather than disappears. This is why rest alone never satisfies.

True rest restores so that movement may continue in new forms. Without meaning, leisure becomes dull, and without contribution, comfort stagnates. The soul grows restless when asked to stop evolving. Retirement belongs to titles, not to essence.

As years pass, the soul seeks depth over speed. Attention sharpens, discernment refines, wisdom gathers weight, and the work becomes subtler, but no less vital. Listening becomes labor, witnessing becomes offering, and presence becomes a gift. The soul's purpose shifts from accumulation to transmission.

Viktor Schauberger observed that life does not move toward rest through stillness, but through ever-refined motion. Energy circulates differently as systems mature, yet circulation remains essential. In nature, what is meaningful transforms. Elders carry pattern, memory, and coherence. The soul seeks transmission until the final breath.

What has been learned longs to be shared, and what has been refined seeks expression through mentoring, creating, tending, and blessing. Life remains participatory. When the soul is ignored, restlessness appears. When the soul is honored, vitality persists, even as form changes. Meaning sustains energy better than stimulation ever could.

Artists often articulate this truth without abstraction. The cellist Pablo Casals, still practicing into his nineties, was once asked why he continued to rehearse. He replied, *"Because I think I am making progress."* This is the soul's posture. Growth does not end with mastery and expression does not cease with recognition. If attention is alive, learning continues. The soul remains engaged to deepen, not prove.

Writers who age honestly speak of this inward shift with clarity. Ursula K. Le Guin reflected, *"The trouble is that we have a bad habit, encouraged by pedants and sophisticates, of considering happiness as something rather stupid."* With age, the soul often releases ambition shaped by noise and reclaims satisfaction rooted in meaning. Contribution becomes quieter and less performative, yet more exact. Joy no longer depends on novelty, but on resonance.

There is no retirement for the soul because growth is beyond employment. This happens in relationship with life, truth, and the unfolding self. As long as breath continues, the soul remains engaged. Not striving or proving but simply participating.

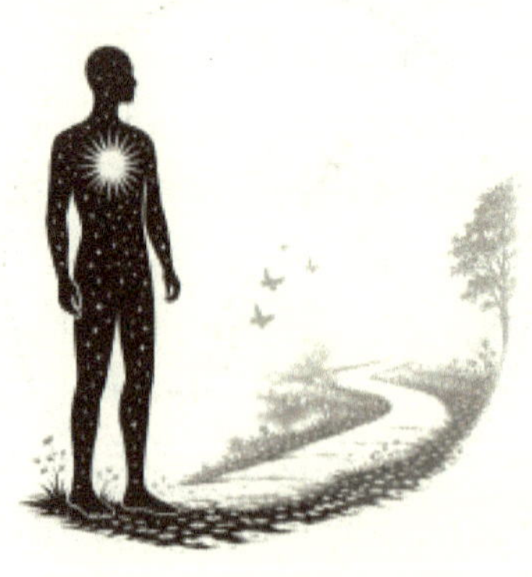

Lesson XXXV: The Gift of Undivided Attention

Teaching begins with how we arrive. Before advice is given, knowledge is shared, or instruction is offered, our presence has already spoken. Our tone is felt and safety is sensed in our demeanor. Attention communicates whether another is seen or managed. Presence teaches without effort.

Daniel Siegel writes, *"Feeling felt is what allows the nervous system to relax."* When a child senses that attention is steady and undistracted, safety deepens and confidence forms. Presence regulates more powerfully than instruction. An attentive father communicates stability without explaining.

A calm nervous system invites calm, grounded posture offers permission to settle, and an attentive gaze restores dignity. These lessons are absorbed long before language enters. This is why the most influential teachers are not always the most articulate. They transmit coherence, their presence carries clarity, and their stillness instructs more effectively than explanation ever could.

Children learn this instinctively, animals respond immediately, and the body recognizes without thought. When presence is fragmented, teaching fractures. When presence is steady, understanding forms naturally. Truth becomes apparent through contact and does not need to be imposed. Presence cannot be faked.

Music sometimes says in a single line what philosophy takes volumes to explain. In *Angel,* one of my favorite artists, Jack Johnson, sings, *"You give me presence with your presence alone."* Presence is the rarest gift because this cannot be purchased or postponed and is undivided attention, offered freely. When I am with my children, I do not measure the moment by productivity or performance. I ask instead: *Am I here fully?* Children require presence, and when given cleanly, this feels like being handed something sacred.

Our authenticity reflects internal alignment and reveals whether words are lived or rehearsed. When presence is incongruent, the body detects the discrepancy. When presence is authentic, trust forms effortlessly. The quality of presence is shaped daily in how breath is held, listening is practiced, and distraction is resisted.

Ancient wisdom carries the same insight in quieter language. Lao Tzu observed, *"The Master does nothing, yet nothing is left undone."* Presence accomplishes without force. When attention is undivided, correction becomes gentle and influence becomes subtle. Children absorb who we are long before they process what we say. To be fully present is to teach without insisting on teaching.

To cultivate presence is to refine influence. This requires integrity more than authority or platform. Every interaction is now an offering and each moment becomes instructional. Even silence teaches when inhabited fully. What remains with others after our interaction is how they felt while being met. Presence leaves residue in nervous systems long after words fade. The greatest teaching demonstrates and does not seek to persuade.

Thich Nhat Hanh wrote, *"The most precious gift we can offer anyone is our attention."* In a world fragmented by devices and urgency, attention becomes devotion. When I choose to be fully present with my children, I am not giving them advice. I am giving them stability, memory, and quiet assurance that nothing matters right now more than their existence.

Among the greatest of all the lessons I have embodied in this life, being present has had a significant impact on my status and the quality of my relationships. Be sure that you implement strategies in your life for getting out of your head and being available when your attentiveness is required.

Lesson XXXVI: Leadership is About Authenticity

The old model of leadership relied on hierarchy. Titles conferred power, roles demanded obedience, and authority was granted externally and enforced through control. That antiquated approach is dissolving.

In place, a quieter form of leadership is emerging that does not command attention but earns trust. This leadership does not dominate. Authenticity has become the new authority. People no longer follow those who speak the loudest or promise the most. They follow those whose lives make sense, words align with actions, and presence feels stable, coherent, and real.

Nelson Mandela embodied leadership as character before command. After decades imprisoned, he emerged without vengeance and explained the discipline required: *"I learned that courage was not the absence of fear, but the triumph over it."*

Authentic leadership demonstrates responsibility in the presence of difficulty. People trust those who have faced themselves, not those who pretend certainty. When a leader owns fear honestly, others find permission to act bravely.

Authenticity arises from lived experience, mistakes metabolized into wisdom, and values tested under pressure. This cannot be manufactured. Authentic leaders present congruence more than perfection. This kind of leadership invites rather than demands.

I learned after having accountability for the lifetime of mistakes I made that when someone lives honestly, permission is granted to others to do the same. If one leads with humility, defenses soften. When clarity is carried without arrogance, influence deepens. Authenticity creates gravity and allures others through example. People feel safe in the presence of someone who is not performing an identity. Safety fosters trust, which allows guidance to land.

George Weah's life showed leadership born from identification with ordinary people rather than separation from them. Rising from poverty to the presidency of Liberia, he reminded his nation, *"Leadership must mean that you are prepared to listen."*

Authentic authority listens before directing. When leaders remember where they came from, guidance becomes grounded and decisions remain human. Influence grows where people feel understood not managed.

The new paradigm does not require followers but cultivates companions. Leadership becomes relational rather than positional and influence flows through consistency rather than command.

The leader walks alongside rather than ahead or above, demonstrating possibility through embodiment. This leadership listens deeply, remains curious, adapts without losing integrity, and acknowledges uncertainty without surrendering direction.

Authority without authenticity collapses under scrutiny. Authenticity without authority reorganizes the field naturally. Leadership is earned daily through how difficulty is met, accountability is held, and others are treated when no benefit is gained. Authentic leaders seek to be aligned, not seen. Visibility follows alignment naturally.

The future will not be led by those who know the most, but by those who live the truth of what they know, whose presence stabilizes others, and whose integrity remains intact under pressure. Leadership is now an inside job, and from that interior alignment, influence spreads quietly, steadily, and without force.

Damien Mander, after leaving military service to protect wildlife, spoke simply: *"The world is changed by ordinary people who choose to care."* Leadership begins where responsibility is accepted personally. No title is required, only consistency between values and action.

Lesson XXXVII: The Most Revolutionary Act Is to Change Ourselves

Revolution is often imagined as confrontation where systems are overturned, structures get dismantled, and enemies are named. The deepest revolution, though, happens without spectacle. When a person becomes internally free, external forces lose their leverage. Circumstances may remain imperfect, unjust, or unresolved but the power to dictate joy dissolves and control collapses quietly. This is the revolution few anticipate.

Revolutionary language has long described this same principle in moral terms. Che Guevara wrote, *"The true revolutionary is guided by great feelings of love."* Without inner transformation, rebellion becomes replacement rather than renewal. When compassion governs action, change stops being reaction and becomes creation. The outer world alters most powerfully when the inner world no longer seeks an enemy to oppose but a truth to embody.

The world feeds on reaction. Outrage, comparison, fear, and urgency keep attention captive. When these hooks no longer land, influence weakens. The system cannot govern what cannot be provoked. This is why for years I have insisted that the best way to end the wars and suffering in the world is for everyone to stop reading the newspapers and watching the NEWS.

Inner transformation changes the rules. A mind trained in presence does not panic easily and a body nourished and rested does not submit to manipulation. If a heart is aligned with values, there is no desire to bargain with despair. Joy becomes sovereign. This sense of happiness does not ignore suffering or injustice but refuses to let suffering define identity and will not outsource peace to conditions that may never cooperate.

Such a person still acts, but from clarity rather than compulsion. Action becomes precise, energy is conserved, and resistance is replaced with discernment. The world notices this stability because of how rare this act of empowerment is. In a culture addicted to reaction, composure becomes radical. In an environment of scarcity thinking, sufficiency disrupts the narrative.

Popular culture sometimes communicates truth more directly than philosophy. In *Man in the Mirror,* Michael Jackson sings, *"If you wanna make the world a better place, take a look at yourself and then make a change."* The lyric endures by removing the distance between problem and participant. Transformation begins where responsibility is accepted personally. When self-examination replaces blame, action becomes immediate and sincere rather than symbolic.

Change spreads when one regulated nervous system alters a room, a single grounded presence steadies a family, and a liberated individual expands possibility for others. The revolution begins the moment joy is reclaimed from circumstance without a need for consensus or permission.

Futurist engineer Jacque Fresco argued that sustainable change cannot arise from protest alone but from redesigned human behavior: *"You cannot change society without changing the values of the people in it."* Systems are extensions of psychology. When perception shifts, behavior reorganizes, and structures gradually follow. The revolution is grown from within until old patterns no longer find participants.

After years of struggling with legal troubles and repeating the same destructive patterns, I learned that if you change yourself deeply enough, the world loses all power to command your inner state. From that freedom, action becomes cleaner, kinder, and more effective. This is the quiet revolution that cannot be stopped.

Lesson XXXVIII: Awakening Begins Within

Ancient Stoics understood awakening as an inward discipline. Marcus Aurelius wrote, *"You have power over your mind, not outside events. Realize this, and you will find strength."* The moment responsibility returns to awareness; conflict begins to soften. External circumstances may remain complex, but inner authority stabilizes response. Awakening begins when attention turns from controlling the world to governing perception.

The new world arrives through coherence. Every transformation that reshapes society begins invisibly, within the inner climate of individuals willing to slow down and listen. Before systems change, perception broadens. Before culture shifts, consciousness settles. Silence is the birthplace.

Mystics described this in experiential language. Rumi observed, *"Yesterday I was clever, so I wanted to change the world. Today I am wise, so I am changing myself."* Wisdom matures through humility. When inner turbulence settles, the urge to force outcomes fades and participation replaces struggle. From this quieter state, influence travels farther.

In the quiet spaces between thoughts, reactivity dissolves, the nervous system exits alarm, and attention gathers. From this stillness, clarity arises and the breath becomes the first act of peace. A steady inhale invites life, and a complete exhale releases urgency. In this rhythm, the body remembers safety and compassion becomes possible.

Forgiveness follows naturally as a release from carrying what no longer serves. The past loosens grip, present regains elasticity, and future opens without demand. This inner work ripples outward. A regulated mind communicates calm, while a softened heart transmits trust, and a present body alters the emotional field entered. Others feel this without explanation.

Contemplative psychology echoes the same truth. Jon Kabat-Zinn wrote, *"Wherever you go, there you are."* No relocation, achievement, or ideology substitutes for presence. Awakening is a shift in relationship to the present moment. When attention stabilizes here, clarity becomes accessible and reaction loosens grip.

The new world requires example. When one person chooses clarity over chaos, the environment shifts subtly. Awakening spreads through resonance rather than recruitment. Compassion for oneself precedes compassion for others. Without this order, burnout replaces service, silence restores balance, and presence renews capacity.

The work remains personal. Those still asleep are earlier versions of the self. Judgment delays awakening, while understanding accelerates the process. To truly awaken, I have learned, we must return to breath, silence, and the body.

From this ground, action becomes clean, speech becomes precise, and choices align effortlessly. The new world is built quietly, moment by moment, through those willing to tend their inner terrain.

Even scientific voices have pointed toward inner coherence as creative power. Max Planck noted, *"I regard consciousness as fundamental."* If awareness precedes form, then transformation must begin at the source. Change expressed inwardly reorganizes behavior outwardly, and this behavior reshapes the environment. The new world grows from individuals willing to refine perception before attempting to rearrange reality.

The same insight appears in quiet spiritual instruction. Ramana Maharshi taught simply, *"Your own Self-realization is the greatest service you can render the world."* When inner confusion clears, actions naturally carry less harm and more clarity and awakening contributes without proclamation.

Lesson XXXIX: Be Rich In Eloquence, Not Force

Force seeks compliance, while articulation invites understanding. Power that relies on volume, dominance, or intimidation exhausts quickly, must be maintained constantly, and breeds resistance rather than coherence. True power moves differently by clarifying, naming, and ordering reality through language.

Articulation is intelligence made audible. When thought is refined, speech becomes clean. When speech is clean, confusion dissolves. Eloquence means precision and is the ability to express truth without excess, distortion, or aggression. Those who articulate well do not overpower.

The Ancients understood speech as a moral act rather than a tool of persuasion. Confucius warned, *"The superior man is modest in his speech, but exceeds in his actions."* Eloquence is not ornamentation but alignment. Words carry authority when they emerge from lived truth. When language outruns reality, trust weakens. When speech is measured, listeners relax and meaning travels farther than force ever could.

A well-chosen word can calm a room while a clear sentence can dissolve conflict. Naming what is happening restores dignity to conversation. Language becomes a stabilizing force. This is why articulation requires responsibility. Words shape nervous systems. They either regulate or inflame. They invite dialogue or shut down communication. Eloquence respects the listener by refusing to waste attention.

To be rich in eloquence is to invest in clarity. I invite you to read deeply, listen carefully, and choose words deliberately. Intelligence matures through articulation and thoughts remain chaotic until language organizes them. What cannot be said clearly cannot be lived coherently.

Lao Tzu wrote, *"He who knows does not speak much; he who speaks much does not know."* Words gain strength through restraint. When language is sparse, listeners lean in. When speech is constant, meaning dissolves into noise. Eloquence is measured by timing. The right word offered at the right moment carries more power than many spoken without awareness. Silence then becomes part of expression, giving language space to land and truth room to be heard.

Articulation also reveals integrity. When words and actions align, trust forms. When language inflates beyond reality, credibility erodes. Eloquence grounded in truth carries weight. Silence, too, is part of articulation. Knowing when not to speak preserves power. Restraint sharpens meaning, presence gives language authority, force demands attention, and articulation earns the spotlight.

Frederick Douglass expressed this principle plainly: *"Power concedes nothing without a demand."* His life showed that the most effective demand is often clarity spoken without hatred. Precision gives courage structure. A clear sentence can accomplish what aggression cannot, by organizing reality rather than escalating conflict.

Marshall Rosenberg, coined as the founder of Nonviolent Communication, taught, *"What others do may be the stimulus of our feelings, but not the cause."* Language that names observation instead of accusation reduces defensiveness and invites understanding. When words illuminate instead of overpowering, dialogue replaces struggle.

In a world saturated with noise, clarity becomes rare. Those who cultivate eloquence offer a gift to themselves and others. I was forever changed when I embodied this principle. I realized life becomes navigable, conflict becomes workable, and understanding deepens when we are exuding eloquence.

Lesson XL: Never Compete with Fools

Your level of competition reveals values. To compete with those uninterested in growth is to accept their terms. The field narrows, standards drop, and energy drains into proving rather than becoming. Victory in such arenas offers little nourishment. Wisdom chooses a different direction.

Fools are defined by their refusal to listen, learn, and evolve. Engaging in their games entangles attention in noise. Arguing lowers altitude and reaction replaces intention. Attention is too valuable to squander. Rather than competing, my invitation to you is to elevate.

Wisdom traditions long warned that engagement with ignorance reshapes the one who engages. In the Biblical book of Proverbs we are directed, *"Do not answer a fool according to his folly, or you yourself will be just like him."* The danger is not losing the argument but losing clarity. When attention drops to the level of reaction, discernment weakens and intention dissolves. Withdrawal, in this sense, is not avoidance but protection of intelligence.

Intelligence expands through curiosity, vocabulary refines perception, and language shapes thought. As words multiply, nuance appears, then understanding deepens, and the world becomes more navigable. Broadening the mind creates distance from trivial conflict.

Legends surrounding Merlin describe a counselor who rarely fought battles directly but altered outcomes through understanding. Later writings attributed to that tradition remind us, *"Wisdom is not proven in debate but in foresight."* The wise step outside of contests that reduce perception. They choose timing, patience, and perspective rather than immediate victory. What appears like retreat is often strategic altitude.

Reading stretches empathy, while listening sharpens discernment. Exposure to diverse ideas strengthens flexibility and growth accelerates when energy is invested inward rather than wasted outward. This is discernment.

Among the Oglala Lakota, Black Elk taught that harmony is preserved by refusing needless conflict: *"Peace comes within the souls of men when they realize their relationship, and oneness with the universe."* A person secure in alignment has little interest in proving superiority. Competing with foolishness seeks validation, while understanding seeks balance.

Choosing not to compete preserves dignity and allows focus to remain on what matters, which includes clarity, integrity, and contribution. Elevation is quiet. No announcement is required or comparison is needed. Progress is revealed through composure, articulation, and depth of response. Those committed to growth recognize one another without argument.

Mark Twain offered this insight in plainer language: *"Never argue with foolish people; they will drag you down to their level and then beat you with experience."* Time spent defending truth against those unwilling to see is time removed from living. Growth accelerates when energy moves toward creation instead of opposition.

Some great advice I offer you is to never compete where growth is absent and never undermine your worth by comparing yourself to others. Compete only with yesterday's level of understanding so today you can accomplish more. When intelligence is elevated, the field widens, possibility replaces conflict, and life becomes less about winning and more about becoming.

Our Obstacles Are Our Allies

Every path is revealed through resistance. What blocks the way sharpens discernment, what slows progress builds endurance, and what challenges our identity clarifies truth. Obstacles are the terrain that shapes the journey. They do not need to be seen as interruptions. Nothing meaningful arrives without friction.

The warrior traditions understood that adversity is not interruption but initiation. Miyamoto Musashi wrote, *"You must understand that there is more than one path to the top of the mountain."* Obstacles force adaptation. They remove rigidity and reveal alternatives unseen from comfort. When the direct route closes, awareness expands. What first appears as obstruction becomes instruction.

An ally does not always feel kind. Sometimes they can apply pressure where growth is required or expose weakness to strengthen. Obstacles arrive with precision, meeting us exactly where attention is needed.

Explorers and mountaineers discovered the same truth through experience. Reinhold Messner observed, *"Mountains are not fair or unfair, they are just dangerous."* Difficulty is neutral until interpreted. When challenge stops being taken personally, intelligence awakens. The obstacle no longer feels hostile but becomes terrain to understand.

Spiritual teachers recognized hardship as refinement rather than punishment. Khalil Gibran wrote, *"Out of suffering have emerged the strongest souls; the most massive characters are seared with scars."* Pressure consolidates identity. When endured consciously, adversity burns away imitation and leaves only what is essential.

The mind often mistakes resistance for opposition, while the soul recognizes this resistance as invitation. Each obstacle asks a question: *Will you respond consciously? Will you refine your approach? Will you grow beyond who you were?*

Avoidance delays this dialogue while engagement completes. When obstacles are met with presence rather than resentment, something shifts. Energy then reorganizes, creativity awakens, strength consolidates, and what once felt adversarial begins to feel instructive.

The obstacle becomes a guide. This does not mean seeking hardship but honoring difficulty, trusting that nothing arises without relevance, and understanding that the path is shaped as much by what resists us as by what supports us.

Life allies with those willing to learn. What stands in the way reveals where capacity must expand, what challenges belief refines conviction, and what tests patience deepens trust. Over time, a quiet realization settles in: *Nothing was sent to stop you. Everything was sent to shape you.*

Philosophy arrives at the same conclusion from another direction. Friedrich Nietzsche wrote, *"He who has a why to live can bear almost any how."* Meaning reorganizes pain. When purpose is clear, resistance becomes material rather than barrier, and what once threatened progress begins to be supportive.

When this understanding arrives, struggle loses edge, fear softens into curiosity, and resistance transforms into relationship. The journey becomes meaningful and this meaning carries us farther than ease ever could.

Life takes time, and time reveals allies everywhere. My reminder to you is that you are empowered by everything and when you trust the redirect and see that things are happening for you and not to you, life will improve from all angles. You are exactly where you are required to be.

Author's Epilogue: Discernment Is Medicine

One of the longest lessons life taught me was not blind rejection, but careful trust. Authority exists, yet authority is not infallibility. Institutions organize knowledge, but organization is not wisdom. I learned slowly that health improves when we stop depending on others to be heathy. No one can inhabit the body on our behalf. Responsibility begins the moment we stop outsourcing awareness.

My life changed when I began asking a different question. Instead of, *"Who will fix me?"*, I asked, *"What is my body asking of me?"* Simplicity returned first in the form of cleaner food, cleaner water, more sunlight, more rest, and more listening. Over time, vitality followed consistency more reliably than intervention. Hippocrates once wrote, *"If someone desires health, one must first ask if they are ready to remove the causes of their illness."* I realized the pills and shots and fast food and doctor's visits were depleting me.

I noticed that many modern habits asked the body to compensate rather than cooperate. Convenience often replaced my nourishment and stimulation drained my energy. The more I removed excess; the more stability appeared. This was a gradual restoration.

Paracelsus observed centuries ago, *"The art of healing comes from nature, not from the physician."* The role of knowledge is guidance, but the work of repair belongs to the organism.

I also learned that fear is often disguised as certainty. We are taught to seek immediate solutions because waiting feels unsafe. When I began supporting rhythm rather than interrupting, resilience increased. This meant discerning when help supports the body or replaces responsibility. As Claude Bernard wrote, *"The constancy of the internal environment is the condition for free life."* Health stabilizes when conditions stabilize.

Clean inputs, such as water, air, light, and food healed me. Removing what burdened my body freed energy that had long been spent managing irritation. I decided to go on a quest, and my mission would be to reclaim my purity. The naturalist John Muir wrote, *"When we try to pick out anything by itself, we find it hitched to everything else in the universe."* Listening became more valuable than reacting.

Over the years, this shifted my relationship to information. I stopped asking what to believe and began asking what to observe. Experience became my teacher and as a result, patterns revealed themselves. My body gave feedback that theory could not override.

I realized much of what I was learning in school and in the university is not factual, reliable, or necessary for my development and well-being. Leonardo da Vinci advised, *"Experience does not err. Only your judgments err by expecting too much."* The organism reports honestly when attention is steady.

Sovereignty of mind and sovereignty of body proved related. When my thoughts slowed, my impulse softened, and when my impulse softened, my habits changed. Health was less a product to acquire and more a state to maintain.

I discovered discipline was not restriction but clarity about what keeps life functioning well. As Marcus Aurelius wrote, *"Look well into thyself; there is a source of strength which will always spring up if thou wilt always look."*

I no longer see health as something granted by systems nor denied by them. Health responds to daily, quiet, and cumulative relationships with what elevates our vitality. Guidance can assist, and knowledge can inform, but attention must remain personal.

The lesson was simple and took years to understand: *wisdom does not live in rejecting authority or obeying blindly, but in learning when to listen outward and when to listen inward.*

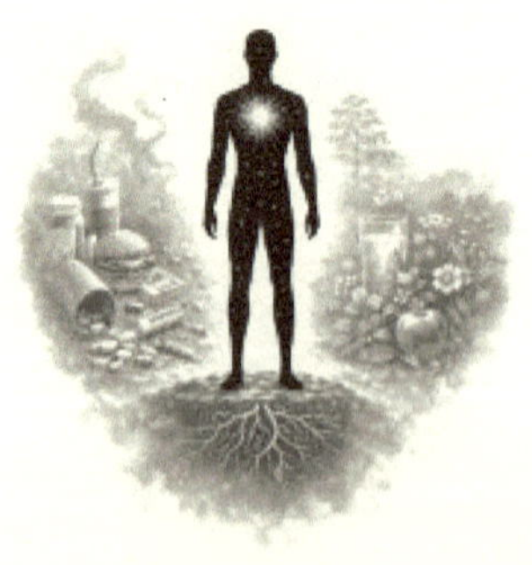

Final Note

I gathered these lessons through years of experiencing the full spectrum of life. While some emerged gently and others arrived through pressure, they all required time. If these pages offered anything of value, remember this not as something new to acquire, but something familiar to reclaim. I do not ask for you to agree with my views or demand adoption with any of what I have written.

What resonates will remain and what does not can be released. Wisdom always knows where to land, and life will continue to teach beyond these pages. New lessons will appear and old ones will deepen. Understanding will shift as circumstances change. This is maturation. Growth refines and does not conclude.

The slow intelligence of becoming has always been recognized by those who studied evolution of both matter and spirit. Pierre Teilhard de Chardin wrote, *"Above all, trust in the slow work of God. We are quite naturally impatient in everything to reach the end without delay."*

This is a call to cooperation with process. Growth ripens through participation, patience, and presence. What is meant to unfold will do so when lived with attention rather than urgency. There is divine orchestration in all we encounter.

My invitation is for you to walk slowly, listen often, stand upright inside uncertainty, and trust the unfolding. Have faith during the pauses as much as the momentum. Trust that clarity arrives when readiness meets attention. Life takes time, and when honored time becomes a teacher.

May these reflections serve as companions rather than answers. May your own lessons meet you exactly when they are needed. May you continue to walk your path with presence, integrity, and quiet courage.

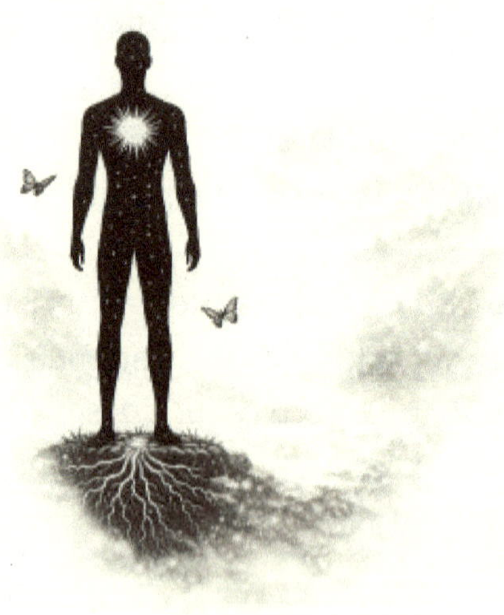

About the Author

Jesse Jacoby is a dedicated father, expressionist, and advocate for compassion, equanimity, and purity. He expends energy adventuring in forests, creating, learning, playing, and writing. He has been following an all organic, fully plant-based, grain-free and alcohol-free lifestyle for fifteen years.

Jesse is the founder and CEO of Soulspire: The Healing Playground (*soulspire.com*). This is a biohacking and purification center with locations near Lake Tahoe in Truckee, CA, and in Nevada City, CA.

Jesse is the author of The Raw Cure: Healing Beyond Medicine (1st & 2nd Editions), The Way Knows, The Meat Effect, Dirty Dairy, You Are Not Powerless, Sovereign Biology, The Frequency Diet, The Unbroken Child, Eating Plant-Based, and several other nonfiction titles. He is a co-founder of Little Manifestors Publishing and has co-authored several kids' books with his children implementing values and raising awareness around compassion and mindfulness.

Substance Shield

Ally of the Aftermath

Substance Shield is a botanical supplement line born from the wisdom of The High Life, a guide for conscious living in a chemically saturated world. Our products exist to support the body's resilience before and after exposure to substances, offering tools of renewal, not judgment. Whether facing pharmaceutical fallout, recreational recovery, or environmental residue, our mission is to replenish what modern life strips away.

Every formula is organic, vegan, wild-harvested, and crafted from whole foods, roots, and ancient botanicals designed to support detoxification pathways, restore depleted micronutrients, and aid in cellular resilience.

www.substanceshield.com
Instagram: @substanceshield

Soulspire is a biohacking and purification offering with centers located in Truckee, CA, and Nevada City, CA which provides each of the biohacking tools suggested in this guide for regenerating the body before and after substance use.

Access the site www.soulspire.com

www.ingramcontent.com/pod-product-compliance
Lightning Source LLC
LaVergne TN
LVHW051004080826
845145LV00009B/2452

* 9 7 8 1 9 6 8 6 6 0 3 9 0 *